Very Close to Pleasure
There's a Sick Cat

THE INDIA LIST

Very Close to Pleasure There's a Sick Cat

and Other Poems

SHAKTI CHATTOPADHYAY

TRANSLATED BY ARUNAVA SINHA

LONDON NEW YORK CALCUTTA

SERIES EDITOR
Arunava Sinha

Seagull Books, 2018

Bengali originals © Meenakshi Chattopadhyay, 2018
English translations © Arunava Sinha, 2018

First published in English by Seagull Books, 2018

ISBN 978 0 8574 2 493 8

British Library Cataloguing-in-Publication Data
A catalogue record for this book is available from the British Library

Typeset and designed by Sunandini Banerjee, Seagull Books, Calcutta, India
Printed and bound by Hyam Enterprises, Calcutta, India

CONTENTS

The Cowherd of the City

Shankha Ghosh

It was the seventh edition of *Krittibas*[1] magazine. The year, 1956. Known as the mouthpiece of the youngest of poets, the magazine's seventh edition saw the addition of a new name: Shakti Chattopadhyay.

It must have happened earlier that a magazine had published a brand-new writer, only to see them disappear over a period of time, or perhaps make a mark slowly, without their first published piece creating a sensation. But those who read poetry had no way of ignoring what this new poet had written, for it seemed to leap upon their senses with its entire being. The positions of words within the flowing prose had been turned upside down, the images rising with a deeply sensual force. Nature seemed to be breathing through the entire composition. There wasn't as much surprise in the line 'immaculate vagina concealed in an undergrowth as soft as velvet'—possibly others could have written the same set of words, in the same sequence—as there was when it was followed by the object of the simile: 'like the

---

1 *Krittibas* is a Bengali poetry magazine, originally edited by poet Sunil Gangopadhyay, which first appeared in Calcutta in 1953 and played a influential role in the city's literary scene in the decades after Indian independence by providing a platform for young, experimental poets, many of whom went on to become luminaries of modern Bengali poetry. Shakti Chattopadhyay also worked as editor of the magazine in the 1960s.

feet of a peasant in the monsoon'. At once the signs of a supple but intricate skill at sculpting caught the eye—the arrival of a new voice, a new mind, became evident. When we keep reading in this poem, which fuses woman and nature, lines such as 'the male in my body touches the heavens', or 'I receive in my body the liquid from the furious, lustrous sky', or 'In every limb of my living body is the consort of my love', it becomes clear that a powerful young poet has appeared, with a deep proclivity for demolishing the accepted way of using words and images. The poem published in *Krittibas* was titled 'The Birth of the Subarnarekha', and the poem held within itself the birth of a love or of a lover, and for the reader it was the birth of a new poet, in that summer of 1956.

On another summer dawn almost 40 years later, that same poet died. In-between there remained almost 2,500 poems collected into 45 volumes, a constant stream of incredibly popular poetry. With this flow extinguished, a line that he had written in another poem published in *Kobita*[2] in that same year, 1956, seemed to have been fulfilled at last: 'Why did you bring me here, take me back.'

Why did he have to be taken back? Who was it who had brought him anyway, and where?

---

2 *Kobita* was a Bengali poetry magazine that, from 1935 to 1961, played a central role in introducing modernism to Bengali poetry. Modelled on Harriet Monroe's celebrated *Poetry* magazine, *Kobita* was published and edited by poet Buddhadeva Bose and featured renowned Bengali poets such as Rabindranath Tagore, Kaji Nazrul Islam and Jibanananda Das.

1

A young boy has come from the village to the city which is waiting with wide-open jaws to consume him. The boy feels unmoored, for 'those who are heartless, those who do not tell the truth, those who do not have minds as open as flowers, those who always have their fists balled up close to their bodies, those who live amid constant noise and unresolved riots between Hindus and Muslims' are the ones who live in cities, who live in Calcutta—he knows this only too well. Perhaps they are to be found everywhere, these people 'whose hearts hold no love, no affection, no stirring of compassion', without whose valuable advice today's world would stand still. There is no attraction anywhere, no desire that anyone feels. Is this detachment 'urbanity', 'modernity'?

The world of rockets and of megatons of destructive power is waiting to be turned into ruins, nowhere on it is the true north to be found, not one sanctuary remains to hold out hope or offer reassurance, and amid all this is our land, our city. All visible grandeur is but external, a patterned shroud over a rotting corpse. Is the mask that conceals everything urbanity, modernity? The boy cannot understand how he will touch this urban, modern Calcutta in his own way, how he will love it, how or from which directions he will 'lay down, like a railway line, a line of love' towards Calcutta. He wants to love, not to lose.

He does not want to lose, but he keeps feeling the city has not accepted him. He has remained primarily a village boy, 'a rusticity purged of perspective' is 'pressing down on him'. But will the village take him back? He had been sent to the city so that he could 'mature', as society put it, so that he could 'grow up', in terms of practicality and pragmatism. Has he grown up? The city has not accepted him, and society has labelled him degenerate. Will he regain his old place if he returns to his village? Will he able to decipher the language of the people if he goes back? Will he not wonder, 'What is this tongue they speak in today?' People no longer seem to understand one another's language, he seems to have become disconnected from everything. Where is his home then? Is it the city of Calcutta, or the village he has left behind? He does not know.

And then an adolescent indignation bristles against a hostile world in which man is perpetually alone, the indignation of not being able to bear this world. Brought face to face with this antagonism and its expansive void, some can be destroyed by its terrible blows, some can take the path of self-destruction, and some can confront them—feel the desire to confront them—with a retaliatory strike. Sometimes the weapon of this retaliation can be anger or derision, and sometimes an intense enlightenment that seeks to rip apart the crude camouflage and discover the truth. But sometimes it is also possible to stand up against these loveless times, so bereft of relationships, to say, See for yourself, love is my only weapon. That is all the boy had wanted to say— it is with this love that he had wanted to demolish the inert configuration of the city, for love was his mission, for 'this bankrupt man has no ability but the one to love'. This was the calling of his soul, which he was afraid of being deflected from, and so 'was trying his utmost to love Calcutta.' With the village he had tried to demolish the city.

This can be the story of any young man or young woman. It can be the story of Nirupam, or of Abani, or of

Nandini in *Raktakarabi*.[3] And most certainly it can be the core of Shakti's—Shakti Chattopadhyay's—entire flow of poetry. His poetry had wanted to demolish the city with the village, demolish death with life, demolish an ageing existence with adolescence.

2

He had wanted to demolish them with the fierceness of a deluge.

We have all read in the epic Ramayana the story of the descent of River Ganga from the heavens. Having flowed as far as Mount Sumeru, Ganga remained trapped in its cavern for a long time and needed the services of the mythical elephant Airabat to be freed. Airabat was very proud of being the one who would split the mountain to free Ganga. Realizing this, Ganga swept the elephant away in her current. Airabat was numbed by the buffeting of the waves.

When I read Shakti's poetry, I am reminded of Airabat being swept away helplessly by the torrents. It is not a matter of one or two poems—if someone were to read his poetry chronologically, or even if one read them in clusters without following chronology, they will have their breath taken away by a succession of waves, by their abundance, their immensity, even their liquid excess. Barely has the reader settled

3 *Raktakarabi* (Red Oleanders, 1924), a complex and symbolic play written by Rabindranath Tagore, deals with the conflict between industrial mechanization and the freedom of human spirit. Nandini, the central character, is often considered a representation of vivacity and undying love.

down after encountering a particular image in a particular poem when another one rushes at them from the opposite point, one that is even more striking. No sooner have they been touched by one gesture of language than a different one appears. Urban as well as pastoral, grave similes as well as earthy colloquialisms, elegant as well as vulgar, imperious as well as modest—all manner of expressions burst out of his poetry with a potent but graceful sinuousness. Such a breathtaking experience has almost never before been offered by Bengali poetry.

The waves keep rolling, often composed of the same body of water, which makes it difficult to distinguish one from the other. One poem is followed by another, and then yet another, leading to a cascade of poetry. It certainly befits Shakti to stand before that cascade and declare, 'Every poet's verse is one long poem—it's just that he writes it in fragments.' Each of these fragments is like a wave in the ocean—just like them, the poems in Shakti's volumes of poetry recede and return to crash upon the shore. We often wrack our brains over the name of a volume of poetry, wondering what it implies about the essence of the book, but here was one poet whose book might not even contain a titular poem. Shakti had written in the introduction to what was almost his last book of poems: 'Although the long poem titled "The Jungle Is in Mourning" features in the book *Here's the Figure in Stone*, I am naming this new book for that old poem.' If we get the line 'The inglorious loneliness of weapons' as a line in a poem in his first poem, it comes to us as the title of a book much later, as does the name 'Calling from the Underworld'. A poem titled 'I'm Happy' will be available long after the book of poems with that name, in the volume titled *Fire of My Reverence*. It's the same story with several other volumes such as *The Flying Throne* and *You Believe in Faith, You Believe in Giraffes Too*. A torrent or a succession of waves—this seems to hold some significance in his poetry.

The metaphor can be extended further. If it's a river we think of, along with its tremendous creative force, we also have to think about the way it meanders across the flatlands, about the way it flows though the countryside, about the way it sends out distributaries in all directions. By now it is much calmer, a great deal more graceful and social.

Shakti's poetry is like this river descending from the mountain peak and flowing through the plains. Despite its internal lyricism, at first it is all-destructive. Then, widening gradually as a current of love, filled with a wistful solitude, it advances through life towards the delta of death. After the mysterious twists and turns on the arduous journey through the heights, this is its natural, effortless movement on the plains, loaded with pain and with fervour, easily acceptable to all kinds of readers.

3

These plains are the extended plains of a land borne along by time. There is the fear of misunderstanding Shakti's poetry unless one carefully observes this stream flowing through the land, through time.

When he began writing, he was determined to demolish things—old ways of using words, old traditions, old values. That the poet is a distinct individual on a pedestal, that poetry is an object to be worshipped from a distance, that it is merely the art of making philosophical statements—these were ideas from which Shakti wanted to turn away. It was to build the mechanism for turning away that he had to declare: 'I blow a gust of untruth into the truth of poetry / the truth of poetry changes in just one day'. Or: 'I drag the truth kicking and screaming to the river / To feel the breeze, then slap it across its face'. It was to build the mechanism for turning away that he had wanted to eliminate the word 'poetry' from his lexicon, that he wanted to say that he wrote not poetry but 'verse'. In other words, even the articulation of the word 'verse' was a powerful weapon for him, suitable for a battle with the socially well-integrated.

There is no doubt that when he began to wield this weapon, he found help in Baudelaire's poetry. This French poet's work, a hundred years after his time, blew into the world of Bengali poetry in the form of a hurricane. It wasn't as though no one had noticed his poetry during these hundred years. Many of them, such as Sri Aurobindo,[4] had commented on his poems, and we had even received fragmented translations of his work. But only after he was translated by Buddhadeva Bose[5] between 1955 and 1958 and published in *Kobita*, and after *Charles Baudelaire: His Poetry* was published in 1961 with an introduction and contextualizing

---

4 Born Aurobindo Ghose in Calcutta, Sri Aurobindo (1872–1950) was an influential Indian nationalist, philosopher, yoga guru, religious leader and writer. Apart from his books on yoga, he is best known for his epic poem *Savitri* (1950–51). He was nominated for the Nobel Prize in Literature in 1943 and the Nobel Peace Prize in 1950.

5 Buddhadeva Bose (1908–74) was one of Bengal's most influential writers of his time. Although he excelled as a novelist, short-story writer, dramatist, translator, critic and literary theorist, he is best known as one of the pioneers of modernism in Bengali poetry. He was the editor and publisher of *Kobita* magazine.

material, could Baudelaire be really said to have arrived in Bengal, escorted by Bose, delayed by almost a century. Shakti was primary among the young poets who were possessed by Baudelaire's work immediately upon its arrival.

It isn't just that Shakti was to write the dedication to his first book as a eulogy to Baudelaire: 'Beloved, most beautiful of all / who is my dazzling salvation', nor that the title of a Baudelaire poem—'I have called out from the underworld' —would emerge as a poem in that volume ('Calling from the Underworld') and, much later, become the title of one his volumes. More important was the change in the fundamental idea of poetry, the change that Baudelaire had wanted to bring to European poetry, a change that was praised by Rimbaud. When Bose referred to an old ideal of the intoxication of mystery, many seemed to discover a new foundation on which modern poetry might be built. 'The invisible must be seen, the inaudible must be heard.' 'One must arrive at the unknown through a gigantic and consciously engineered catastrophe of the sense organs.' 'Each and every process of love, sorrow and madness must be mastered.' 'One must search for oneself, one must absorb every drop of poison.' 'It is necessary to experience indescribable agony and miraculous power, it is necessary to be severely afflicted, to be repulsively vile, to be utterly infernal, to be the crown jewel of pundits.' It was as though a manifesto was written for the poetry of a new era—or so thought some individuals living in a crumbling, despairing, disorderly, post-Independence Bengal. And so did Shakti. Which was why he had to write: 'I distract myself with art and allure, an inert body sick with malice'; 'Germs of an incipient illness, worms, pus, bleeding / Are all things that love me well'; 'Terrible beauty, look, sin, oh, dazzling sin'; or that famous line: 'Who knows whether poison isn't the real drink / And nectar the venom.'

This is the time when, in the words of Shakti's self-projection Nirupam, 'Allen's *Howl* has been translated into Bengali. We've read both the English and Bangla versions. We've read other fragments of poetry besides *Howl*. We've read about them. We've learnt quite a lot about them by now.' Allen Ginsberg has even arrived in Calcutta with his heady poetic techniques and lifestyle, and Shakti and his companions are consorting with him closely. 'We have just the one weapon against this world bound for destruction, and that is our creativity'—a new circle of poets is making waves in America with this credo while *Howl* is being banned in San Francisco on grounds of obscenity.

This is the time when a new phrase is about to be coined in Calcutta's literary circles: the Hungry Generation. The Angry Young Men of Britain and the Beat Generation of the US had inevitably appeared in one of the Shakti's pieces but, in order to convey the distinctiveness of this particular movement, Shakti had written at the outset: 'The social environment in those countries is one of affluence, they can be Beat or Angry. But we are Hungry. It must be termed a hunger for any form or aesthetic. No form or aesthetic can be left out . . . the main thing about this revolution is that it is omnivorous.'

Yet, this is also the time when, along with Baudelaire and Rimbaud from the nineteenth century, twentieth-century names such as those of Rilke or Jiménez have reached the young poets. The first English translation of Jiménez's gentle *Platero and I* has already appeared in 1957, entrancing some in Calcutta soon afterwards. Addressing a silver-grey donkey who is his companion, the Spanish poet talks of a hypnotic, illusory world, each of his lines brimming with a sombre silence. And Shakti too draws Platero directly into his poetry, alongside his other hard-hitting poems, writing, 'Platero is mine and I too am not without Platero / Does our god sit in the west dangling his legs?' 'I, too, Platero, want to kiss you for a long time / To descend to the place in the heart where the god lives.'

And so Baudelaire or the Hungry Generation remained only a starting point for Shakti—they could not have become the primary force of his poetry. The imminent revolution with the word 'Hungry' in its name, one that would seek 'to destroy the conspiratorial positioning of material objects', one that would wish to 'dance in ecstasy on the corpse of modernity', was not one with which Shakti would be directly connected, therefore, and his work would soon become unacceptable even to the Hungry poets. Once upon a time he had said: 'Poetry is a sort of private and solitary sexual act for poets. Poetry is deeply unsocial.' But this too was only his preparatory period. During this period, as Shakti himself did not hesitate to acknowledge, he had received an education in 'imagery' and in 'romanticism' from his contemporary Ananda Bagchi, while from Alokeranjan Dasgupta he had learnt 'rhythm, wit, and an apparently liquid Bangla'. And he had invariably mentioned Jibanananda Das,[6] being one of those who had discovered

---

6 Widely regarded as the foremost Bengali poet of the post-Tagore era, Jibanananda Das (1899–1954) was also a novelist, essayist, literary critic and professor of English literature. His masterpiece *Banalata Sen* (1942) is often considered the finest collection of modern Bengali poetry.

and adopted Jibanananda as the most important poet in the Bengali language. But all of this were the preliminary ingredients used in the process of developing himself consciously. Eventually, Shakti matured himself through a variety of poetry from home and abroad, modern and old, his poetic personality being formed by the pull of the internal lyric, although there was a constant link with Bengal's villages. Especially notable in his confessions is that he says he had not had to 'read every word to understand' Jibanananda's poetic sensibility. Since he had not felt this need, the nature of Shakti's poetry grew distant from that of Jibanananda despite the fact that he had stood for a while at the older poet's doorstep. And in order to create this distance, the primary technique Shakti applied at the core of his poetry was the use of melody, the touch of music. That is why one or two lines, sometimes an entire stanza, keep recurring in his poetry with a noticeable distinctiveness, like a refrain. That is why his poetry is often configured like a song, as if only awaiting melody, such as this well-known one brimming with the pique of unrequited love:

> I shan't go in there what's that you've worn on your
>   brow
> I shan't go in there
>
> The very last star has melted the sky shan't find it
>   any more
> You can use force but the heart shan't go in there
>   any more
> The boy still picks flowers what's that you've worn
>   on your brow
> When is the time right for it?

Everyone grows older why don't I instead of being
    a little boy
Why is the calm and tranquil heart around me
    foaming on the current
Your face is so beautiful what's that you've worn
    covering your brow
I don't know it, I know some of it too for ever

Reading such poems makes it obvious that Tagore's songs would inevitably fill Shakti's life, and the force within the latter's verses; even the connection of his poetry to his essential self would be created by the Bengal of the songs of Chandidas[7] and Ramprasad[8] and those of the Bauls.[9]

Does this mean the accents and idioms of some of the aforementioned poets or their poetry can be identified in Shakti's work? Sometimes they might, but that is not the point. The point is that the expression of heartfelt grief,

---

7 Chandidas was a Bengali poet (or several of them—it remains inconclusive) from around the thirteenth to fifteenth centuries. His poetry, associated with the Hindu Vaishnava movement of Middle Bengal, depicts the love of Lord Krishna and his consort Radha. Chandidas' pastoral drama *Sri Krishna Kirtana Kabya* is regarded as the most significant work of Medieval Bengali literature.

8 Ramprasad Sen (*c*.1720–81) was a saint, poet and singer associated with the Hindu Shakta cult of Bengal, whose songs—generally addressed to Goddess Kali—are still widely performed. Ramprasad is credited with creating a new compositional form that combined folk music with raga-based classical melodies, which greatly changed the sound of Bengali music.

9 The Bauls are an order of religious singers of Bengal known for the freedom and spontaneity of their mystical verse. Their songs often deal with the love between the human personality and a personal God who resides within the individual. Rabindranath Tagore was one of many Bengali poets who acknowledged a debt to Baul verse and music.

unbridled submission yet an addictive, maddening love with which those poets could draw the people of the land easily to their lyrics, that undercurrent of mystical passion is inseparably intertwined with Shakti's poetry. This allure even leads to a profound role of God in his poetry, which is expressed not just in titles such as 'God Lives in the Water' but also in an indistinct—almost ghostly—aura that repeatedly envelops him. In fact, this poet announces directly: 'I believe in a certain kind of God. A God who is an elder, who listens to what I have to say, who makes me listen . . . The "he"-s and "you"-s in my verses are largely addressed to him.' The heartfelt grief, the unbridled submission, the addictive, maddening love that I was referring to are melded with a divine passion which enables Shakti's poetry to transcend the mere 'modern'. Journeying along this path, he joins the mainstream of a Bengal that has existed for ever; this is where the currents of his poetry flow directly across the river of time though which the country has passed. Under the pressure of urbanity and modernism, under the complexity of the intellect and the incomprehensibilities of the philosophy of truth, poetry seemed to have been limiting the frontiers of its readership, but the very frontiers that we had considered the destiny of contemporary literature turned out to be fragile under the force of Shakti's poetry. And it is through the demolition of these borders that our rhymes and rhythms have been resurrected by his poetry, by his hands.

Shortly before his death, Shakti was in Santiniketan[10] to teach poetry and while formulating a plan to awaken a

---

10 A town in north-central West Bengal, home to Visva-Bharati University, founded by Tagore in 1921 as a basis for a common fellowship between the cultures of East and West.

love for poetry in young people, his first thoughts were about rhythm. Did he not know that his students would already have studied rhythm as a 'subject' within the standard syllabus? He couldn't possibly have been in the dark about this. But why did he still want to talk to them about it? One of the reasons might have been a desire to demonstrate that rhythm had taken new shape in his—and some of his fellow travellers'—recent work. But I doubt whether that was the only reason. I suspect that within his thoughts there lurked the idea of eliciting a love for poetry through a love for rhyme—he may have felt that through rhythm it was possible to arrive at the everyday eternal.

It was assumed, as many still do today, that rhyme in poetry is antique, laughable and worthy of abandoning, as though it is fundamentally incompatible with whatever is modern. At one time, it was a widespread belief that it is prose which is the primary or even only recourse, that prose alone can touch our natural selves. And yet, it was a young poet who had raised the question during Tagore's centenary celebrations in 1961: What form might the future of rhythm take in our poetry? 'The rhythm may not be that of Ramprasad, but what prevents it from being a free form of that rhythm?' he had asked. There was indeed no barrier to this any more. The answer to this question seemed to flow incessantly over the next few decades from Shakti's poetry, in one lyric after another, in lines that passed from lips to lips like proverbs:

> Schopenhauer had thought
> There was nothing the heart brought
> For there was no time for anything
> And so all morning, desire

Is giving me the courage to conspire
What if I were to start flying?

Or

I remembered, I remembered you
The whistle at the junction just blew
At the level crossing stands the train
And are you, right now, reading Hart Crane?

Or

But your key is very safe with me
Though only now have I found the time—
Write me if thou wishest to have it back.

This last line gives us a brand-new shock. 'Write me if
thou wishest to have it back'? What was casual a moment
ago—'Though only now have I found the time'—has sud-
denly acquired a classical, even archaic, tone? How can the
sublime and the profane come together so beautifully? An
appreciation of poetry makes it clear that a 'wish' instead
of a 'wishest' would make the line collapse—in that 'wishest'
is lovingly hidden the key to the poem. But how does some-
one have the courage to use such language? Even though
he knew that no one would touch this archaic version of the
language now, he went on to use it with ease in many of his
poems, perhaps with indulgence from Jibanananda.

In his novel *A Place to Stand On*, we read a few things
about the writing practices of the young. There's a passage:
'Kalyan writes prose poems. Nanda recited four sonnets.
Marvellously constructed. Only Barun objected to the use
of classic forms of verbs. I said, There's no discordant

note—what's the problem?' Surely we recognize both Barun and the narrator here. Just as Barun's objection is understandable from the point of view of a modern sensibility, so too is the narrator's response: There's no discordant note—what's the problem? Of course, this might only be a partial answer. Having no objections is one thing; bringing forth a distinctive flavour through the use of the classical to break the mould of the popularly modern is quite another. The role of archaic phrases in Shakti's poetry would perform this task—it would break through the shell of the modern to journey towards its heart.

4

But journey towards which heart? Forging a link with an older Bengali is not the same as adopting that older Bengali, after all. A tangled game was playing out in the town of hearts, and Shakti's poetry seeks itself within itself, amid the tangled modern. If it cannot find itself, it rushes out, goes far away, searching for its own image in the city, in the forest, returning with the mourning cry of not having found it. 'Had I then locked him up before setting out to look for him outside? Strange!' This is the last line of the novel *Abani, Are You Home*? Are you home, anyone? No one answers, only the knocking of the night is heard in the sleeping neighbourhood, behind the barred doors. 'Abani, are you home?' This was how he looked for himself, or for God within himself, who, 'when I walk across Chowringhee at midnight or run like a lunatic along the tram lines, is with me'. Maybe he isn't there always, sometimes there's the feeling, 'Why did my father leave me behind and go off alone?'

It is thus that many sections of his poetry, even his novels, are filled with his own stories, his personal joys and sorrows. Many novels have shades of autobiography in them, but Shakti does not offer the opportunity for such 'discoveries' in his novels. These pieces have such unself-consciously detailed autobiographical elements that readers do not need to discover them. One of the qualities of new-age poetry, some have said, is the poet's confessions. There is nothing else to think about in poetry besides sex and death, the poet has no responsibility but to explore and expose themselves, only the personal is sacred—some poets had tried to adopt these ideas as their core beliefs. So had Shakti. That's why his poetry and his fiction are two adja-cent forms of autobiography. In the book *Parashuram's Axe*, Shakti has prepared commentaries on some of his own poetry. We can pick up similar commentaries from his novels as well. Nirupam is bewildered because Jamuna has gone so far as to invite him to her wedding. Atanu says, 'What does it matter? It will improve your writing.' Nirupam does borrow a sheet of paper and write, 'I shan't go in there / What's that you've worn on your brow / I shan't go in there.' The one who's turned him down says, 'It's better to suffer. It will bring forth poetry. But it will destroy your life.' Nirupam completes the poem, but then feels hesitant: 'You don't think it's too personal?' His friend reassures him: 'It's bound to be a little personal.' Yes, it's bound to be, but 'isn't it a little childish too?' 'That it is, a little,' the friend says. But he also adds, 'That's what's special about your writing.'

So it is not just the history of what has been written but also its nature that we learn directly from the writer himself. He knows his poetry is redolent with his 'personal' voice, the voice of his adolescence; at the same time, he also knows that it is this childishness that is the attraction of his work—the fun of it.

Because all of Shakti's poetry is sprinkled with elements of autobiography, we become familiar, through his writings, with the coming-of-age of a man. Even if his fragments of prose or the books labelled novels had not existed, we would have had no difficulty in capturing the entire picture from his poetry alone. 'Why did my father leave me behind and go off alone?' With this secret regret, 'the poet seeks a poem in desperately calm silence'. Someone is changing bit by bit through all this. 'As he changes / A man stops abruptly, holding his hand out to life'. There was a time when 'Ripe hooch every day / A pot of poison darkened by dreams of destruction / Shakti would drain it, not a bad state of affairs'. But today? 'Today everyone's a legend.' Today he can ask, 'Can I be called an alcoholic any more?' Today he wonders, 'Just floating about / Suspended in festivities / Will it be possible to live again?' Whether it is possible or not, yet 'With greater pride than everyone else I live alone'. In this loneliness 'Within me weeps / The deceptively complexioned child, rejoicing in death'. As he grows older, he wonders 'When did people call you a young poet? At what age must you screech to a halt in order to look beautiful?' Not that he ever screeches to a halt, he keeps on writing, but he also realizes that 'A slackness has entered the way I live / The swiftness of the senses is not as swift any more'. We are conscious of internal bleeding. Does he remember that at the age of thirty, this poet's destiny had made him say: 'The young poet is God, the aged poet is an old nuisance and, in a word, a tramp'? He realizes it today, and can say easily in his customary confessional manner:

> He's finished, even hearing this leaves not a scratch
> On the skin, I hear, and turn over for aristocratic
>   rest.
> No more can I offer distinguished guests in the
>   auditorium
> The ferocious heat of a poem completed last
>   night.
> Old, former pieces are wrapped in ancient
>   odours—
> I read them out to gain some meagre satisfaction!
> I am not well, circumstances create a pressure—
> It's time to go, it's best to go before fading away.

The account and self-pity in this poem titled 'It's Time to Go' may even remind us of a few of Tagore's laments in his final days. The mysteriousness that Shakti considered the greatest hallmark of poetry is not to be found here, only in 'aristocratic rest' will Shakti's old voice be heard briefly. Despite all this, his astonishing courage, his courage to confess, to present himself without a shield lives on even in this poem.

5

And so Shakti Chattopadhyay's poetry is a search for himself in the world, in nature, in some personal god. His poetry then is a projection of his autobiography on the canvas of a real person. Are there signs of the times in his poetry then? Any symbols of society? How often has this poet boasted at different places: 'I am unsocial'? He has tried to stay away from 'dirty politics' and concluded that it is not his job to ensure the well-being of the people of the world. He has understood that other forms of literature might have social work as its mission, but 'poetry has no actual objective.' When it is only a current of consciousness with indistinct contours and no particular subject that flows through his poetry, radiating multiple beams, how will we identify any signs of the times?

Nor must we. But, at least through Shakti's poetry, we do find a route to that sociological time in which he wrote. Does this route lie in the fact that sometimes his poetry—even when it turns away from politics and sociology—does allow some signs of contemporary tragedy to rise to its surface? This does happen. One can easily talk of 'Bloodstains', when the sight of a 'Dazzling, stupefied body of a headless youth' forces the poet to ask with a straightforward simplicity, 'Why this gruesome massacre', and to grieve, 'Not for himself, but in asking for a revolution he is guilty.' It can be asserted that this poet has heard the call for a cataclysmic revolution 'at the door, beneath the stairs, on the glaring afternoon street / at gatherings of armed and unarmed people'. We can talk of his memories of refugees from the time 'Al Mahmud has taken leave of the alleys of Calcutta', when 'we acknowledge Bengal has a free, magical sky / across the Padma'.[11]

---

11 River Padma is the main channel of River Ganga in Bangladesh. The river is often used as a symbol of Bangladesh (earlier East Pakistan), which was carved out during the Partition of 1947 from the greater province of Bengal, thereby creating an unnatural border through a land of a common language and customs.

He changes, changes constantly. But does this changing mean that Shakti has gone too far away? Not exactly, for even when he is close to the final outcome of his *ouevre*, this is not a fundamental aspect of his poetry; rather, it is the occasional visit of the unexpected. Not through these—his eagerness about the world outside is evident, instead, in an internal, compassionate voice, a voice in which he can write, almost like lyrics for a song: 'Humans are weeping so much be a human and stand by them / . . . Humans are so lonely come and stand by them.' The repetitive refrain of 'I am alone so alone' is set aside then. A bird does get a view of the river eventually, but 'in the city humans burn alone in vain'. Should we leave the city then and go into the forest? From a distance it appears that 'Calcutta is the sweetness of his world-girding sorrow.' Through such wishes to create relationships, and also a lack of relationships, we will observe another face of the poet. It is not just personal; it signifies a different kind of love which has become as multi-directional as the wind and whose appeal can make us say, 'It seems love has become easier at this age.' He had one day seen postmen in the autumnal forest, he had seen the distance growing between one letter and another, between one human and another. But he has 'never seen the distance between trees grow'. If we combine with this his constant desire to turn into a tree —'wherever I go set down roots, branches sprout, tendrils sway in the breeze'—we see a different structure for viewing human relationships. The gap between humans grows, the desire to close the gap by distributing letters intensifies; he wishes to say, 'make me the postman for all old letters,' for he has seen the 'beautiful lying down beside me like a man'. 'If the love within humans is emptied out', it will be 'greater even than death'. So he wants to draw the human cooperative to that melancholy joy where the beautiful is not isolated. The countenance of this simplest of loves is the social rebellion in his poetry, the revolt of love against non-love. And so in rebellion he wanders on the streets, in cities and in forests, he keeps talking of leaving, he says one should not look back when departing. But while he avers 'I must not look back', and does in fact proceed without being waylaid by petty intricacies, his poetry is replete with images of looking back. 'Memory is nothing but poison. Who wants to be infected by this poison?' This is what he wrote in his novel *I Am Leaving*.

The sentence did not end there, though: 'Who wants to be infected by this poison, besides Nirupam?' Whenever the subject of leaving comes up in Nirupam's thoughts or in Shakti's poetry, images appear from villages, dripping the poison of memory, and he is possessed by the age he was when he lived there. An age that makes him determined to 'turn the village, the forest, the habitations upside down / all of it, all of it'. He will certainly break away from what people have turned their cities into, he will go wherever his fancy takes him. But not this time with a Platero from a distant land as company. He will desire 'to leave on the back of a buffalo', he will feel 'I want to take him on my back, too, one day', and if he discovers poetry, 'I will hang poetry from the trees here'. The beautiful will then take its place beside humans, there will be no antidote to the fatigue of walking the streets of civilization besides creativity, which will become the true companion of humans, and this love-soaked dream is what Shakti Chattopadhyay's poetry is.

Externally, constant references to death and departure provide an agonizing appeal to his poetry, but within it lies a frantic desire to remain involved, 'because I will leave by myself and with others within the circle', since 'the meaning of life is search, not death, only explosions'. Announcing that he was going away from everyone, Nirupam had said one day, at the end of *I Am Leaving*, that he was 'leaving behind the city, the villages, to the blue light amid the stars in that sky, to become another star', he had said, 'none of you will be able to hurt me any more'. In that blue light, we will see the face of a man with the radiance of a child in motion: crafted yet natural, bewildered yet engrossed, addicted yet indifferent. Walking the streets, that man sings only the unending song of the young cowherd, brimming with the tangled games of the town of hearts.

Originally published as 'Introduction' in *Collected Poetry of Shakti Chattopadhyay*, *Volume Seven* (Calcutta: Ananda Publishers). Translated by Arunava Sinha and reproduced here with kind permission of the author and the publisher.

O Love O Silence

(1960)

In Four Parts

I shall not live very long I do not wish to live
I shall take in the wondrous sight when the grain ripens
I have settled my subjects in my home in the near darkness
I'll take some things for some time, I do not wish to live long

I shan't take futile steps towards this incomparable world
Desire is so stormy I do not know its destination
Does the heart ever know when a woman makes you hers?
Still I shall not live very long I do not wish to live

Only a scene, let he who wants to dig down to the core
The floating river float the boat now float the boat
Youth goes and so shall I—diver or peasant, live unharmed
Like determined leeches in your field, in the world

Oh I shall not live very long I do not wish to live
Who will seek the sun-filled flame or eternal rain?
Inexperience widens the world, deepens the peace
When ancient I shan't sing a dirge I do not wish to sing

Does the Garden Know Each of Its Trees?

I worry how the enormous garden will remember
Birds visit every tree, every sorrow is as delicious
As succulent fruits warmed respectfully by light
I worry about the mind
That wants to pluck from the tree and pick from the ground
It's brought baskets to gather pleasure in huge amounts
I grow old, now I see that
The fruit flushed by a radiant glow isn't within reach at all

You Believe in Faith, You Believe in Giraffes Too

(1965)

I Remembered

I remembered, I remembered you
The whistle at the junction just blew
At the level crossing stands the train
And are you, right now, reading Hart Crane?
A hundred-mile journey was made
But your study grant is small, you said
This way you will never save a bit
It's true my pocket's got a hole in it
But you had a brainwave very soon
Under slanted beams from the moon
Here, you said, take this instead
Now your photo's kept beneath my bed
I remember, I remember you
The whistle at the junction just blew
At the level crossing stands the train
Are you reading, just like that, Hart Crane?

Did You, in the Garden, Take My Hand?

Did you, in the garden, take my hand?
On that day, when you took my hand
Suddenly this heart was filled
With every wonder
That was the time of carnage
That was the victory of creation
In your hand lies the power of travel
Does that please your heart?
Does it circle the world and return
On a memorable breeze in spring?
Still there is no respite this time
The rooster rolls its crest from side to side
Hours pass—blood soaks my breast
Did you, in the garden, take my hand?
Did you, in the garden, take my hand?

Evening Has Fallen Now

Evening has fallen now. You have hammered rock all day
In the arms of the mountain
The July rains have ended in the sal forest
Your fist isn't clenched any more
It won't be wrong to take a break
Why not go abroad
This year, say the things that you have not

How slow the clouds of August are!
A fever runs through you
Flowing, hot
This year, say the things that you have not

Evening has fallen now. The bustle of the day is done.
I will surrender my silent head to your breast
Green stems and flowers
The world makes errors
It will, for ever
Can evening purify it now or is it never?

You had loved everything
Feelings famed for separation
The hum

Of wisps of memory—or is it song
Usurps all of me
You have hammered rock all day
In the arms of the mountain
The July rains have ended in the sal forest
Still agony has not turned you crimson
To every part of my body came errors
One by one, I am spent
With fatigue. Everyone eyes me with contempt

Abani, Are You Home?

Bolted doors, the neighbourhood sleeps still
All I hear is the knocking of the night
'Abani, are you home?'

Here it rains all the year round
Like grazing herds the clouds here drift
The green blades of grass look away
To choke my door
'Abani, are you home?'

Heart half-suffused with an ache
Bound for afar I fall asleep
To hear the sudden knocking of the night
'Abani, are you home?'

The Key

Even now I have it with me
Your favourite key, which you lost
How do you unlock your trunk now?

Is the mole still on your chin?
Will you visit a new land, my heart?
I had to write to you suddenly

But your key is very safe with me
Though only now have I found the time
Write me if thou wishest to have it back

Hiding in irrelevant memories
I see your face, bright with tears
Write me if thou wishest to have it back

Sarojini Had Realized

Afternoon, a darkened room—a floor-shrouded wide sky
Sarojini steals a white swan and takes it away
Perhaps it will rain, perhaps a hard wind will blow
Did Sarojini hide the flame of the mouth in the clouds?
The white swans had been ambling alone in the field
Saroj was at home—all she did was gaze wide-eyed at them
At all these swans—when she saw it was about to rain
She went out and was caught in the swan song—fabric love
All she did was gaze wide-eyed, this swan was not for touching
Sarojini had realized this—only, her heart had not

Town of Hearts

It was still dark at the time
Still light in some parts
A tangled game was playing out
In the town of hearts

The riverside had all but sunk
Half-dissolved in the skies
The moon just shone with gentle grace
And unforgiving eyes

What use is it passing her
When her frown can lock
All the doors with warning signs
And set guards round the clock

What use is it calling her
It's over once it starts
The tangled game of carelessness
In the town of hearts

I Have Murdered the Golden Fly

(1967)

Here in This Foreign Land

It all suits this foreign land
Drainpipe trousers, jungle-print shirts
Immaculate kerchief round the throat, if Ashwathama is
    with you
It all suits this foreign land

Briar pipe, pointed-toe shoes
The pretext of sunlight on dark glasses clamped on the nose
It all suits this foreign land

But your malacca cane—
That cloud-laden home in your heart
Where you went to start the rest of your life
Is where you were reassured today

It all suits this foreign land

Not a Very Happy Time, Not a Very Joyous Time

Tottering from head to toe, from wall to wall, from parapet
    to parapet, swapping pavements at midnight
On the way home, a home in a home, feet in feet
Breast in breast
Nothing more—a lot more?—even earlier
Tottering from head to toe, from wall to wall, from parapet
    to parapet, swapping pavements at midnight
On the way home, a home in a home, feet in feet, breast
    in breast
Nothing more.
'Hands up'—raise them high—till someone picks you up
Another black van in a black van, and yet another
A row of windows, doors, a graveyard—skeletons lying
    awry
White termite in the bones, life in the termite, death in life
    —therefore
Death in death
Nothing more.
'Hands up'—raise them high—till someone picks you up
Throws you out of the van, but into another one
Where someone waits all the time—clutching plaster like
    a banyan seed
Someone or other, whom you don't know

Waits behind the trees like a hardy bud
Holding a golden cobweb noose, he will
Garland you—your wedding will be at midnight, when
    pavements are swapped, tottering from head to toe
From wall to wall, from parapet to parapet
Imagine the train waiting while the station runs, starlight
    by the dying bulbs
Imagine the shoes walking while the feet are still—heaven
    and hell turned upside down
Imagine children trotting to the crematorium bearing the
    corpse—in afterlife
Decrepit men dancing horizontally at a wedding

Not a very happy time, not a very joyous time
That's when
Tottering from head to toe, from wall to wall, from parapet
    to parapet, swapping pavements at midnight
On the way home, a home in a home, feet in feet, breast
    in breast
Nothing more.

The Hinterland

There was a particular kind of garment I had sought from you
At that moment through the window, on the grass covering
 the graves in the cemetery
The rise and fall, the demolition of love had intensified
Our consolation—we have still not forgotten each other
Our consolation—the pollen had risen as love inside the flower
Our consolation—one day I had wanted to sing for you on the
 riverbank

I never went to a factory as workmen do
There was a particular kind of garment I had sought from you
After a long time spent inert like a tree, vivacious like blood
I was submerged beneath the weight of successive layers of
 clouds on my shoulder
The way the pebbles part company with the waterfall
The way the melody forsakes the lyrics of a song
Was the way my heart felt the constant desire to leave
Over these they left across the grass covering the graves
For somewhere unknown

We have even had days when our hours have passed without
 our eyes flickering
We have even had days when we have turned the only
 language we knew upside down

We have even had days when both of us, speaking,
Have been fulfilled in the green, unrippling grass
Our days together days together days together
Such an age-old spring has come an age-old spring
It was the garment of this spring that I had sought from you
Everyone has taken gifts matching their desire from you
Our days together days together days together
We have even had days when our hours have passed without
our eyes flickering
We have even had days when we have turned the only
language we knew upside down
We have even had days when we have been to the mason to
say
Make us a house of brick and mortar
Give us lights, give us fans, give us a canopy—we're getting
married tomorrow

There was a particular kind of garment I had sought from
you
That was when uncertainty, deflected off its path like a grain
of barley
Had leant over us to say
Give me alms give me alms give me alms
Allow yourselves to experience sorrow
To drift away on past glory like phosphorus on the waves at
night
Give me alms give me alms give me alms

That was when the footprints on the grass covering the
graves in the cemetery

Had awoken to race towards the person who had walked by

That was when the shed flowers had risen upwards towards
the branches

That was when the old cracks had reappeared to claim the
new bridge

Whenever we want authority we have to pay a penalty for
unauthorized entry

I can never go towards the garment, naked

The way the unclothed moon goes up to the clouds is not
how I can go

The way the heart goes up to sorrow is not how I can go

The way dreams go up to the sleeper is not how I can go

I only gaze at the rise and fall and the demolition

Of the enchanted love of my youth

On the grass on the graves in the cemetery

For a long time I have not seen an explosion of words in
your letters

For a long time I have not rubbed my nose on your face to
breathe in your fragrance

For a long time I have not been able to create waves in the
pitchers on your breast

For a long time I have not launched your face in the water

For a long time the train has not left the station

For a long time the night wind has not raced across the fields
with the yellow ticket in its breast

For a long time I have not found an explosion of words in
your letters

Postmen in the Autumnal Forest

(1968)

Postmen in the Autumnal Forest

I have seen postmen wandering in the autumnal forest
Their yellow sacks filled with grass like swollen sheep bellies
So many letters new and old they had found
Those postmen in the autumnal forest
I have seen them pecking away incessantly
Like a solitary crane at a fish
So impossibly, mysteriously, warily absorbed
They're not like those postmen of ours
From whose hands our constant, indulgent love letters
Are lost all the time

We are moving away from one another continuously
Distancing ourselves out of greed for letters
We are getting many letters from far away
We are going away from you at once to hand over letters
Loaded with love to the postmen

And so we are moving away from the kind of people
We are ourselves
And so we are about to express our foolish weaknesses
And motives, everything
We can no longer see ourselves in the mirror
We keep floating in the unpopulated evening veranda

And so we are taking off our clothes to be swept away
Alone in the moonlight
For a long time we have not embraced one another
For a long time we have not savoured human kisses
For a long time we have not heard people sing
For a long time we have not seen babbling children

We are drifting towards a forest even more ancient than the
    forest
Where the mark of eternal leaves is fused in stone jaws
We are floating away to a land of such unearthly connections
I have seen postmen wandering in the autumnal forest
Their yellow sacks filled with grass like swollen sheep bellies
So many letters new and old they had found
Those postmen in the autumnal forest
The distance between letters has only grown
I have never seen the distance between trees grow

Moving House

I am terribly afraid of moving house
To lose the ancient dingy lane I've known for ever
Many people do love those wide and open streets
Asphalt roads, Palm Avenue
Swimming in the breeze like cotton balls
Beneath these newly installed blue lights
Unlike many others I don't approve of them
My style is to be dressed in poverty, head to toe
To wear a pair of torn-and-tattered trousers
I'm an old-fashioned man as well
I cross the Calcutta Maidan in the rains
Barefoot, boots in hand, trousers rolled to the knees
What you people refer to as original
Is not what I am either
I cannot hide my habits and borrow money
I repair the shoes and clean the bathroom
The lord of the ration card—that's me too
I don't even baulk at adding the rejected 'Sri'

Anyway, back to what I was saying—about homes
I have suddenly moved house, my hidden wish—

Use this newfound place for my suicide
No old things will cajole me here, there's nothing
For me to miss, so who can stop my unhindered death?

The Quilt Border and the Mud Hut

(1971)

Try Just Once

Try just once to love
You'll see rocks tumbling from the breast of the fish in the river
Rocks rocks rocks and the river and ocean water
Blue rocks turning red, red rocks blue
Try just once to love

It's good to have a few rocks in your heart—they echo sounds
When every walking trail is treacherous, I can arrange the rocks
    one after another
And go all the way to the distant door of autumn's pale stars for
    a look
At the naked use of poetry, of waves, of Kumortuli's idols in
    gaudy, sequinned, embroidered costumes.

It's good to have a few rocks in your heart
There's no such thing as a letterbox—leaving it in the cracks in
    the rocks is good enough
The heart does want to build a home sometimes.

The rocks in the breast of the fish are slowly occupying our hearts
We need it all. We shall build houses—erect a permanent pillar
    to civilization.
The silver fish left, shedding rocks
Try just once to love.

All of Us

All morning some people told us stories of our lost days
All morning some people did not tell us to leave
They only said, sit here and listen, all of you
Those days of yours which you had left behind
No one picked them up
Lose your money and someone will pick it up behind you
Lose your way and people will be marching down that very
    road
Leave a corpse behind—vultures, jackals will savour the
    flesh
Leave the door open—frightened women will collect brass
    utensils
Leave your home behind—it's intangible, all intangible
You have discarded your torn shirt
Your broken lantern, old papers, letters, leaves—
There's someone to pick them all up
You cannot pick up those days that you have lost
The more you eat the closer you will go to death
Everyone will explain—that's life, that's fulfilment, that's
    the entire body
That's what's called society, duty, literature, devotion,
    meaningful grief

All morning some people told us stories of our lost days
They did not tell is where they got them
They did not confess whether they had stolen, from the
      streets,
Our lost dreams and memories
They told us those incomparable dreams and memories
      from the lost days
We felt once more those lost stories
Which had been lost to us all this time
Lost in the woods fields old notebooks slates village fairs
In rivers seas beaches roads talkie show houses
Lost at the station ferry in Calcutta in villages
In someone's hair in someone's face in someone's eyes in
      someone's promises—
We have lost them lost them lost them—we will not get
      them back
We know, never
Get back those days replete with storms rain sunshine
      autumn
Those childhood days of nakedness tears a little money
Won't get them back
Won't get back the days of launching paper boats the roar
Of the short-lived ocean in the yard
Won't get back again won't get back again won't get back
      again
Those days of the moonlight fallen leaves mythical tales
All morning some people kept telling us stories
Of those lost days of ours

And so we did no work all morning

We listened to the stories of our lost days in silence till
eternity

Like policemen

We finalized our course of action like policemen

We considered retrieving those lost days of ours

By despatching police dogs

Thus we kept ourselves occupied with dreams of such

Tumultuous possibilities

Thus we crossed the uphill and downhill passages of time
one by one

When they said, 'Your wagon is here get in get in

If you stay here tigers will eat you'

At once we leapt some crawled some walked

Towards the cart taking us to the future

All of us escaped the jaws of the tiger here to travel towards

The jaws of the tiger there

Sonnets

(1972)

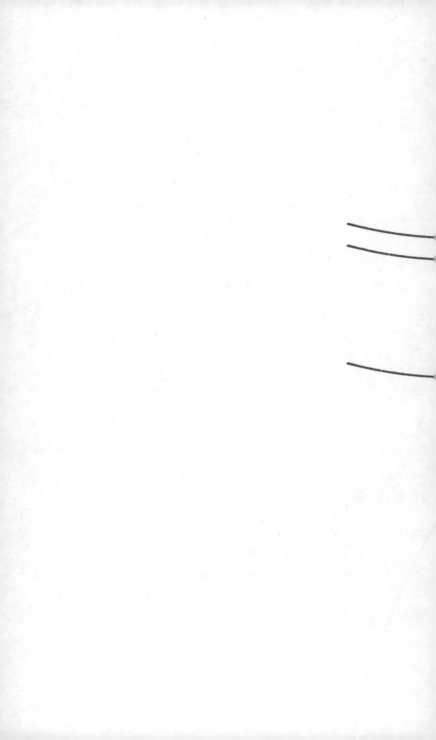

Eleven

Platero, I envy you, my darling, for a very long time
You have slept next to my heart, on your back
You have eaten up my roses, the notebooks of poetry
Brimming with the future—a memorable flock of kerchiefs
Still I did not stop you, only warned myself
Like fathers do. Sometimes I went to a distant land
Will you never bear again, will I, alone, bear the weight
Of memory and sorrow, and, moreover, of you, all day?
Listen to tales of travel—tales that are not very old—
Your strange gaze fell on my face now and then
In an instance you directed me towards a new poem
So much love in daily life drenched in our poetry
Still, Platero, an enchantress keeps tempting me inside
The more you unravel, my darling, the more I get snarled

Twenty-Six

All night long the policemen pursued us, for
We three idiots were the only witnesses present
To the murder of the sun on the dead river's bank
A perfect fit for this obscene investigation
Directionless from a screaming pain in the arse
So Calcutta will see an uncontested culling of animals?
Setting up of industry? Moneylending for beggars?
Auspicious objects will be imported, apprentice
The barest minimum of phone towers will be planted
On mountains, unconquered peaks, if any, will be conquered
'But what about people?' A group of poets is agitating
The waters of a pond—fools, thieves, scoundrels
Never learnt reverence, only wrote reams of poetry
Whom was it that we three poets observed suddenly?

Thirty-One

Many jasmines of the night have I seen, I do not wish
To see any jasmines in this life, let the jasmines see
Let them gaze deeply at me as they fall to earth
I will never look at anything, I will drown to death
I have seen many zebras play, but not the plundered
Museum zebra, I know the brush on its miraculous body
Was shed. His expression did not suggest the attention
Of death and memory, only the struggle of the living.
So I belong to the jasmine, never to the medlar
Night jasmines drift down on the clock, the yellow stalks
Lend motion to the frozen hand of the past moment
And so I belong to the jasmine, to courtesy, to excessiveness
And so I am the night jasmine's, only at the jasmine do I gaze
I will not look anywhere else, I will drown to death

Thirty-Seven

Moheen's horses have not returned to Moheen's home
They are grazing by the zebras. Twenty-two zebras
The horses are lurching in a black sea of tumult
Like needles of time, those horses and those zebras
Like obedient ghosts under the infinite glow of the moon
They wander—they talk—who knows what they say
It does seem to me they will not return to humankind
I have more thoughts but I cannot utter them
Are the twenty-two zebras not zebras then? Could they even
Be ornamented ships in this ghostly oceanic moonlight?
Is that a coconut that bears the dwarf's melancholy?
Will the moving images prance out of our sight?
Are those Moheen's horses? Are they not our zebras?
All form is shed under the light of the miracle

Forty-One

Platero has come to love me, I have loved him too
Our days are not nights, nights are not days
The sun rolls appropriately from east to west
From his red sphere like the red paint lining the sole
Drops our—Platero's and mine's—silent love
Platero, you come with me too, I cannot urinate alone
Some people intimidate me, make mysterious threats
It is quite pleasant to be a little cowardly from childhood
They had loved me so much—brought me flowers
Bought me a hat, from the seaside, a whip made from
The tail of a fish—a multitude of gifts
I have not forgotten them childishly, have I?
Platero is mine and I too am not without Platero
Does our god sit in the west dangling his legs?

Sixty-Three

If love comes I'll turn things upside down and leave
Go where my whims lead me—they love to travel
If love comes why should I need a royal feast?
For years I'll eat the food of the poor with joy
If love comes I'll tear off these charming covers
To leap and run in the glare of the scorching sun
'Idiot,' the beggar hungry for comfort will shout
If a slap on the face isn't enough, a kick in the arse
If love comes I know all this will happen. If I don't
Have you, will I sit in silence? Will I not scream?
Will I not create bedlam, but just sit in defeated rage?
If I get no love will I live my days as now
Like a thief, or in lamentation, distracted?
Love alone knows how badly I want love

Seventy-Seven

There's a particular handkerchief I can never find
I have entered the women's compartment to look for it
Sometimes I have taken the tram to the nurses' quarters
I have looked for it everywhere with Manash's sister
I have hovered near the women students' hostel every day
For the cause of just this treacherous handkerchief
Disaster has befallen me, I have overcome it, and yet
I have entered the privacy of the shopkeeper in the shop
After a long time I found only at this midnight past
The handkerchief at the other end has begun looking for me
I have not heard whether it has gone down or up the street
Its search, unfortunately, will be without the help of men
I have flown many a kite and balloon and gift in the sky
I have also wandered a great deal near the handkerchief

Eighty-Nine

Perhaps the dust has gathered on my desk in the darkness
I do not sense its presence, I feel everything will
Be visible when the light returns—right now, the hill
Covers the adjoining land—the church tower rises nearby.
This is the way of faith—like a connection between
Hearing and the lips felt over the phone—beyond the eyes
Sans taste, smell, colour, or is it a related trip
To heaven, though the hill covers the real adjoining land
Dust does no harm, nor does it grow—it isn't personal
Not usable, not edible either, just an eyesore
How does dust gather relentlessly, all day and night
Where there are animation, existence, and brooms too?
Dust gathers in daylight as well—it can be possessive
Indolence weighs me down, free me of dust, woman.

My Lord, I Become Tarnished

(1972)

My Lord, I Become Tarnished

Over and over I become tarnished
Lord, make me pure
So that it's the cage which
People buy, Lord, I become tarnished
Over and over I become tarnished
Make me pure just once
Lord, if living is the
Primary thing, my Lord, I become tarnished

The Tiger

As soon as he remembered on a cloudy afternoon
The tiger of eternal love went out in the forest . . .
I saw him, I went up to him, I said to him: eat
With gummy eyes, rooted to the spot, he wouldn't move

And so I felt a terrible fright, for his eyes floated laughingly
In a blue happiness, on wing and on fire, in light and in dark
The tiger was thickset, glum-faced, a mountain of resentment . . .
His beauty flowered beneath the raking nails of my tiny hand

As soon as he remembered on a cloudy afternoon
The tiger of eternal love went out in the forest . . .
I saw him, I went up to him, I said to him: eat
With gummy eyes, rooted to the spot, he wouldn't move

A Mistake Somewhere

There has definitely been a mistake somewhere
Millions wander around Calcutta with a primary illness
Despite this spring has been here for some time now
Evident in the flame of the forest, the frangipani nose-ring
There has definitely been a mistake somewhere
In behaviour.

Man has lost everything to retain violence in the heart
Love and ardour have gone, turning into blood disease
Stupefied, capable of killing
There has definitely been a mistake somewhere
In behaviour.

The company of humans is no longer justified
Bile from a dog is probably sweeter.

If Sorrow

If sorrow makes a mistake I'll take it to the forest
And leave it with the tall trees on which
There are neither thorns nor flowers, no welcome.
Not by themselves, small people are saddened by
Their own sorrow. I'm smallish too, who knows why
With me sorrow deviated from its straightforward way

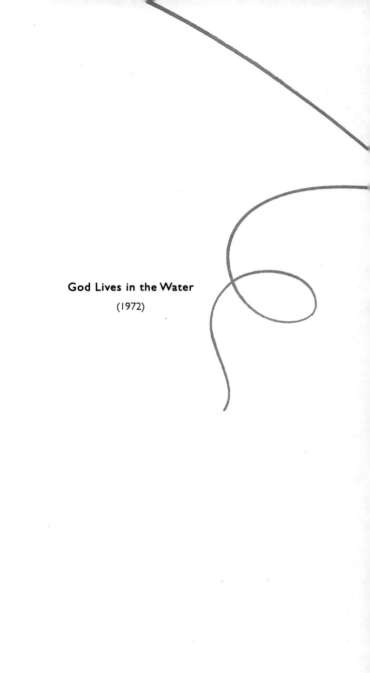

God Lives in the Water

(1972)

The Search

Who's in the red house?
A heartbeat, perhaps?
Are there people here?
Or is it haunted?
Will I find him ten feet below earth?
Will I find him twenty feet below earth?

Don't Go There Again

Ringing on the distant phone
Barbed wire
Don't go there again

Don't go there again
You're fine here
Two cats, black and white
In your hands
We'll talk, you and I
Do you remember still?
From the distant phone comes the ring
Of barbed wire
Don't go there again
Don't go there again

I'm Happy

(1974)

Sorrow

If the poet feels sorrow, so can Calcutta
Yet everyone says, we've never seen anyone so cruel
Deceitful, cunning, malevolent, heartless, lustful,
The crone even yanks children away from their home
To grind them beneath wheels, murder them, throw
The hapless poor into a drain, can Calcutta feel sorrow?
I know it can, Calcutta cries its heart out
Deep within, you just have to listen closely
At midnight lay your ears on the deserted asphalt
You will hear someone weeping, secret sighs of sadness
Like clouds rumbling every day from a deep cavern
Can someone who must always weep know how to feel sorrow?

One or Two Words

With just one of two words I mesmerize people
I am the genuine nationalist
All of you are fake, you've deceived
Which is why none of you has received
Bouquets of fresh grass
I am the genuine nationalist

When I find a man is dead
I use a sword to sever his head
That's enough to make the people afraid
And my aim is unwavering
I am the genuine nationalist

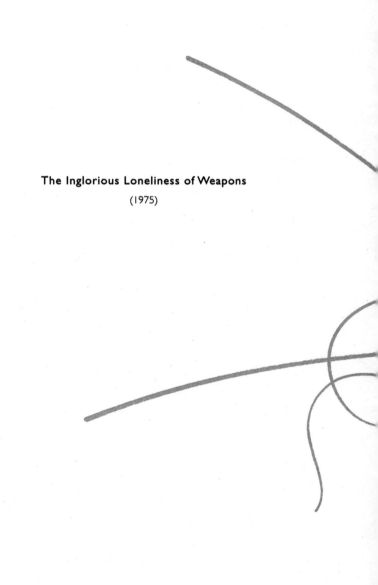

The Inglorious Loneliness of Weapons

(1975)

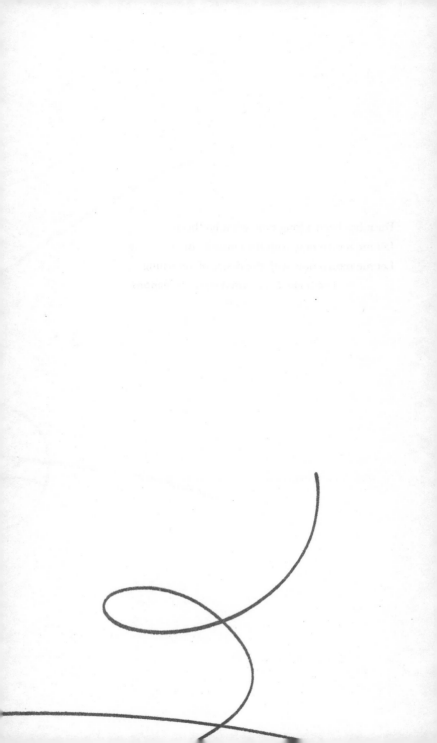

Let Me Return Now

Let me return now with the curiosity of returning
Let me return now with the desire of returning
For it has been a long time yes it has been
Let me return now with the curiosity of returning
Let me return now with the desire of returning
For it has been a long time alas a very long time
At home in the day and in the day at home
The water sweeps away the clouds of the night
I must give myself a very hard warning
When you come you can warn all the others
Will you misremember all your mistakes
But I am in love with all your mistakes
Let me return now when it is time to return
Let me return now with the desire of returning
At home in the day the night clouds gather
At home in the night the day's clouds are gone

For a While

Calcutta burns beneath the sun, dust flying in the searing wind
Amid this the gulmohar casts a shadow of honey and passion
The young man and woman sit by the lake with the swans
Carelessly plunging their faces into feathers
Once, you were attached to this scene, to me, woman
You were in Calcutta, you were near me, next to me
Today I mourn the fiery fate of that Calcutta
How are the two of you so calm under the scorching sun?
Unmoved by the dust storm, unmoved by your urban labour
Where did you acquire the divinity of rocklike stillness
How long have you been sitting this way—do you not age?
Would you like it if I sat beside the two of you
For a while?

The Burning Handkerchief

(1975)

The Burning Handkerchief

The burning handkerchief lay very close to the heart
Its flames licking at the fair face like a lunatic
Licking and biting, on its tongue coagulates
Tasty skin, freezing blood, ribs brimming with
The touch of the breast. When love dwindles within a human
It's called a rock, sun and shadow climb face to face
Like a straight tree felled and abandoned by the river
A prolonged abandonment deeper than a man's death

I Have Done All of Manisha's Tasks . . .

I have done all of Manisha's tasks since childhood
She cannot do any of them
Sunk in natural, inert sleep, face down in languor
She lies with her back to the sky, her pose is lovely
Still she was terribly startled on seeing me one night
There was lightning in her, meaning Manisha's, naked body
Giving off flashes. And I, a sorry figure, drenched in rain.

Fragments

(1975)

Five

If ever I visit the other side of clouds
I could take you along too
After which, there's no road. Flower beacons are lit
Will you burn something? Won't you light the evening lamp?
We have to go farther
The way is hard, harsh

And amid all this, erratic winds
Tell me, calmness, who came here?

Thirteen

It's her the face reminds me of
Whom does the face remind me of?

Fifteen

There's no rain, I think it had rained
In the dazzling sunlight many have seen him waste away
Many have seen him flee across the field
To where there are no humans, only stone and nature
No sharply cutting wind, only a slow gentle breeze
That's where
There's no rain, I think it had rained

Nineteen

Take a step down if you want to stand by me
Take a step up if you want to stand by me
Stretch your arms out, cut your ties to the world out there
One step up and one step down, if you want to stand by me

Twenty-Two

So many ruses to gather shells
The shells still hold blue water
Grains of fulfilled sand
Keep gathering in the course of living
Does anyone ever imagine
Their days will pass gathering shells?

Twenty-Nine

On the parapet the cat wails, it can be heard at times
Sometimes the crow weeps deep in its chilling sleep
Missing something they sought, people grow wary
In this aimless lane and sob constantly in the dark
There's enough of the fire
There's kindling
There's duty
There's no rice at all, not even the scent of rice

Fifty-Three

Not this way, it doesn't work this way
Raindrops on the river, not the mountain
Not this way, it doesn't work this way
Which way then? How does it work?
How do both the fragrance and the breeze
Always hover close to the flower?
That's the way, it does work this way

Eighty-Eight

And now these feet
Want to hit the street
But the road is now a stream
Can't I be a fish in a dream?

Eighty-Nine

Overhead, the sky is burning
A raging wind is blowing free
I am afraid of the sunshine
Is that why you're holding me?

One Hundred and Five

Let me pay a visit to the garden
There are some wilted blooms
Let me pick them
Someone else is to blame, not she
At the time they fell from the trees
She wasn't nearby
She is to blame
Let me see, if I can
I'll go tomorrow too
To pick you, wilted blooms

One Hundred and Seven

So many birds in the sky
I wrap myself in a shawl
You know why? Your kisses, all
Turned me
Into a bird one day
I flew, came back too
Now, I am genuinely afraid
I wrap myself in a shawl
What if I go, what if they call
I am afraid

The moon is lying on the road, pick it up
Like a signal, put it in the black parting of
The hair of the jungle, stand on the mountain
Yourself, on the peak, the sky will ask
Take this road in silence, you will meet it
There are trees, birds, the moon in the water
Bury your face in your placid palms over there
You will catch a glimpse, if you want to

The moon is lying in the water, pick it up

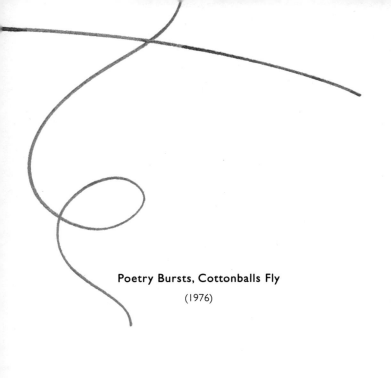

Poetry Bursts, Cottonballs Fly

(1976)

Why Should I Go?

When it rains I want to dissolve in the rainwater
And enter the earth sprawled beneath, the soil
But how should I go? And why, for that matter?

Yesterday was spent in the sky, I had to swim
In the evening wind like a bird to a village
Behind the leaves on the trees by the river there
I could have forgotten my human ways to become a bird

Should I abandon all this to enter the earth, the soil?
But how should I go? And why, for that matter?

River Breaking Banks

The river's breaking both banks, the river's widening
In the middle is the twisting, turning water, above it
Clouds are gathering. There's no escape, no crossing
If you hear the water roar before the afternoon ends
You'll know that the river's hunger isn't satiated
The river will eat a lot, it will keep eating a lot
Keep an escape route open in case you need it
You'll have to get away, and, when escaping, you
Mustn't look back, for then there will be no doubt
About it. You and everyone and everything will be drowned

I Slash Rhythm and the Woven Net

(1976)

Taking Advantage of My Absence

Taking advantage of my absence Calcutta destroys itself
    every time
Everywhere I look—the roads race over houses and walls
    with broken ribs
Taking advantage of my absence Calcutta destroys itself
    every time
The sky collapses on Calcutta, the Shaheed Minar is
    pulverized, the Ganga dies
Everywhere I look—Calcutta has taken sufficient revenge on
    itself
When the beautiful wants to ravage itself, perhaps this is
    how it does it.

I only give you time away from me, I do not leave you—why
Have you not learnt to understand this even now?
I only give you time away from me, I do not leave you
Age has caught up with me, I must confront myself now
It will be a busy time afterwards, the bell will sound in the
    palace
The carriage will appear at the door—
And within my reach then will be the time to go—just the
    time to go

I only give you time away from me, I do not leave you—why
Have you not learnt to understand this even now?

Burying my face in Calcutta's destroyed chest I have wept a
    lot once
The way the rainclouds weep is the way I have wept a lot once
For someone to whom the darkness and light are identical now
There are no shadows anywhere anymore
The high porticos and low, the automobiles, the newspapers
    are all gone
Like a transferred stationmaster it has destroyed all the old
    places
And gone away to a new station somewhere else—

Taking advantage of my absence Calcutta destroys itself
    every time

Ritwik, for You

You are safe now, death can no longer threaten you
It won't cast a long shadow on the distance at your door
Won't break your bones, your home—his ascetic world now
Will do nothing that bears the sinful touch of humankind
Because it was there you tried to provide whatever there was not
The fullness of the goat and the echo of emptiness were
    yours alone
Whatever was spartan was intense in the stone when it
    existed
In beauty and in heart, in your wayward manic soul
Trust and fear lived together—once troubled, Bengal is
    reassured
No one else is there now to torment with lightning
    whiplashes
This mediocrity, this wealth, this satisfaction within people
You have left, audacity has departed, humility has arrived
You languish like burnt stones here by our side in Bengal,
Ritwik, for you the insignificant poet cries in grief

Just One Wave

Slipping out of the grasp of the sea, just one wave
Has arrived in my yard where it lies like a snake
In the wriggling moonlight. On this cloudnight the moon
Trembles like a thief behind the leaves at the sight
People no longer have to fear this waveserpent
For they have seen it break ranks when it came
Neatly deserting the team, smashing the rhythm,
Alone, to a corner of the yard, like a tired woman

Here I Am, in Stone

(1977)

A Terrible Battle In and Out

After all my wandering I'd meant to go to you
My easterly wind
But whenever I talk of going
Where's the weapon, asks my pen
And in the bower, in the vines
The bloodstained moon has hidden now
Longing eyes and wistful face
A terrible battle rages in and outside you, my easterly wind

A Mountain of Leaves

Like leaves from a tree sounds have gathered in the yard
There's no wind, and so there's a mountain of them now
No one climbs it, no trees grow, there's no invasion
Of bird or beast, no waterfall or restless stream
And so the leaves pile up in the yard uninterrupted
There's probably no one at home—no children here
Else the mountain would have been shattered into pieces

To Someone Else

This is not meant for you, but for the one
With whom you're living in happiness and peace
Listen closely, my dear young man so tender
That woman was never in love with a dying oven
She likes the man who'll be awake day and night
Sitting by her head, not at her feet. She has never
Liked the man whose childhood keeps returning
On some pretext, even after saying it is leaving
The only thing by way of identity was this
If the brown leaves fall to the ground
What's the message for you, young man?
Is it one of love? You're so tender

Calling from the Underworld

I'm calling from the underworld, can you hear my words?
I'm calling from the underworld, can you hear my call?
Come now, from that sky of yours to me beneath the earth

Come and stand near me, let your feet burn in my heat
Let your hands burn, let your soft buttery body burn
To black, defile it, hold me . . . the underworld is agony

From the peak climb down the roots to alight on my face
On my breast, on my happiness, on my sorrowful nails
The dirt beneath them is the earth that I've clawed out

I'm calling from the underworld, can you hear my words?
I'm calling from the underworld, can you hear my call?
Come now, from your very own sky to me beneath the earth

Come and stand near me, the underworld is agony
And my love for you is lurking within me

Parashuram's Axe

(1978)

Our Relationship

God lives in water
For him I must one day
Dig a lake in the garden

I am alone
Let god be near, that's what I want—let him live in water

He needs the peace of water, so I've understood
Living close by makes long relationships with humans
Impossible, so I'm told
But he's not a human
Besides, even if he lives in a distant
Garden, the empty distance too
Will save our relationship

The Illness

I have an acute illness now
My hair standing on end, lice in my scalp
Millions of ravenous ants in the undergrowth

The rain will be late
It will be very late
I enjoy frightening people now
All I enjoy is frightening people

The Flying Throne

(1978)

Between the Ass and the Jungle, the Moon

Once, I only had to close my eyes to see
An ass and a moon walking through the jungle in silence
Neither turning to look at the other
You have named this walking together in time . . . love.

I don't understand such relationships
With many people I have walked many times
Just like the ass and the moon
In wordless silence
None of them has even touched me

Still I only have to close my eyes to see
An ass climbing up the sky
And a moon walking in the jungle
In sum, their change of positions is important to me.

The Way People Cry

Endlessly I stand on one foot, as at a public meeting
A blue flag on a bamboo pole—I stand alone the same way
Trussed up as though I'm the Shaheed Minar piercing
    the sky
And so the fault is mine, I'm inspired, ambitious
You have pointed out my blemish—of what miserliness
Have you left a hint on the stairs, you're such a tyrant—
Which way do I go? Both up and down, or is it your intent
To live on the path with no passers-by? Then it's
    intermediate
Melancholy, let me tell a story now, with the craft
Of storytelling, of the beauteous captivating heartbreak
That it's wrapped in, freeze—in solitude, when did you ever
Offer company on one leg? Even the water flows sceptically

Is that bad? Intermediate melancholy weighs the boat down
I stand alone as before, obedient, a dilettante
For all his flaws, he is wrapped in a single virtue
On voyages he always took me along for company

People Are Weeping

(1978)

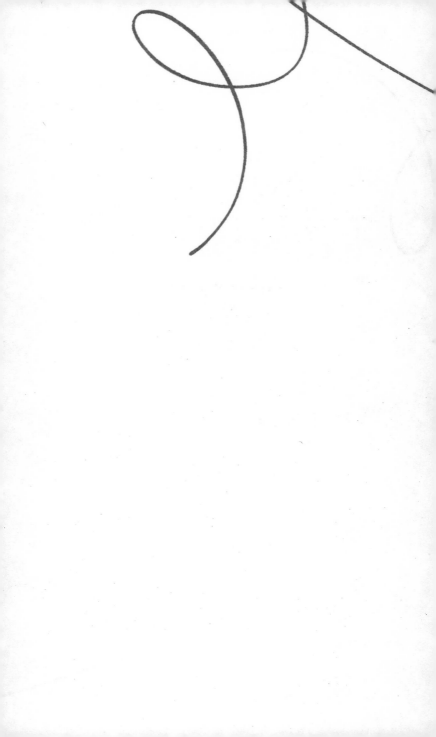

Take Me, Tree

If I could enter a tree just once in my life
Hide myself within, even for a moment, I'm willing
A single moment alone, not in water but in wood and stone,
Wood that makes no promises will take me as its own
With this trifling desire I have long been visiting
The forest by night, in the darkness. Lost myself
Holding a root by the hand I have wanted to go inside
Where there is a road, and a solitary traveller

Take me, tree, take me even if momentarily
Within you I will see restrained growth
You're not silent like stone, there's amity
There's pleasure, affection, love, consideration
Take me, tree, take me even if momentarily

The Letter

You've left home, since my letter's been returned
You're not there, the house stands, with a rusted lock
The peon has brought the letter back—for you've left
You must have found another house at a fair price
Send the address, how many rooms, is there enough light?
Have you put the plants in the veranda, do they bloom?
Tell me all, write me in your crooked script
A letter, it won't be returned, I'm alive

All of This

Shed a blood-drop from your heart, from your heart
Let it fall upon my breast, my arid breast
Plant a tree with flowers
Plant a tree with fruits
—I shall need all of this
—I shall love all of this
The blackness of your ghostlike form in the dark
I shall love it, really love it
Shed a sudden drop of blood from your heart
That is all I need
Let it fall upon my breast, my arid breast
Add a fragrance to the wind
—I shall love all of this
—I shall need all of this
—I shall love all of this

Allowed to Leave

Seven days since I left my old home
And settled down here in the new one
A little, not myself, that will take time
Packing everything, it seemed not everything
Can be taken, you have to leave behind
Not some household objects, but the wind
Over the house, happy memories, stains
On the wall, such things.
Now it will be whitewashed, my remembrance
Will escape secretly, it is not to be preserved
I have moved with two children who need preservation
The first has left, telling me, not even telling me,
Who has to be allowed to leave, and why

I've Entered the Forest

You smell of jasmine, don't come near me
The scent of flowers, jasmine, don't come close
Don't come near, hide behind the trees
I have my axe, you know, I've entered the forest
I've come in to chop wood, not to gaze
Pain becalmed, I've cut your magic bond
Severed all the chains, it's not too late
I have my axe, listen, I've entered the forest

The Way People Cry

Do birds and beasts cry the way people cry?
I am alone I am so alone, alone within myself,
Alone in the forest, alone at home and abroad
By day and night, in joy and sorrow
No shade, no blade, no flowers in the garden
A slope like a waterfall—hair flowing on the back
A fullness of clouds, no water, a celebration in water
No grain, no strain—there is dry straw, collapsed
Foliage, like earth that has subsided underfoot
All this emptiness fills up this land

Still people live, because there is death they live
Death is not life, not continuity in any form
They live in crowds, live in solitude, in company
They live, they stay alive—because they must live
Do birds and beasts cry the way people cry?
I am alone, still I am alone

When Flints Are Struck There Will Be Bloodshed

From Mikir Hills the elephants come down late at night
Tea gardens below, the shade-giving trees shed leaves
Clouds hang from the dark brown branches all in a row
The bungalow beneath. Even lower, the dishevelled waterfall

I sit in a corner of the veranda, watching the west
In case something catches my eye or misses my eye
With this hope I sit here, sit here watching the west
Silent like rocks in a corner of the veranda

At dawn I'll see my reflection in blue water and leave
I may never return, from Mikir Hills the elephants
Will come down late at night in single file, like rocks
When flints are struck there will be bloodshed in the veranda

The Rain on Calcutta's Breast

We hadn't asked for it, still the rain, like galloping hooves
Rang out on the tin shed, flowers were sprinkled on the road
A stain trickled down the garbage hillock, a different
Black torrent facing ugly houses instead of bungalows
Of Calcutta, the rain came, the rain flooded the bylanes
Swept away stories, rags, fish scales and peel, everything
The humidity in middle-class homes, insurance policies on
Strewn scraps of paper, voting ballots, dry wood shavings—
All of these. From the rain to the picnic in the rain, all of it
Is useful for Calcutta, dead grass—that's useful too
The labour room on one side, crematorium ashes on the other
Birth and death, all the details, are neatly arrayed in the rain
In a satin case inevitable lumps of cottonwool rest
The rain goes to bed a little late on Calcutta's breast

Something Left

Not for the rocks, nor for the stream or waterfall
I come here because I love the branches
With the desire to stand beneath them
And look up, I come here
I love
The dust on the green leaves
The flowers
I come whenever I can
I realize the leaves have been shed
Something else has grown
I lower my head
And stand for a while
Then I go back home
Was there something left to see?
Was there something left to see?

Want To

The sound of such a flower's name
Made me want to open my doors wide
The farm is full of flowers in the bud
And her hair is spread out like a cloud
The sound of such a woman's name
Made me want to open my doors wide

No More

No more of these dying flames
Burying, this way,
       The fire in the sand
Revolution
Summon them
       At once
Pull out by the roots
       The people, blood-smeared
       People
No more of these dying flames
Burying, this way,
       The fire in the sand
Make haste, let us enter
       The arms, the roads, the veins

Today

He'll need a stretch of low land to sleep
Make his bed below the pomegranate tree
Give him a woven mat, even if it's tattered
He'll need a stretch of low land to sleep

Pile some bricks for his exhausted head
Draw his arms to his chest and cross them
Make a mound of earth beneath his ankles
He'll need a stretch of low land to sleep

Remember to put a lamp by his bed
In the carefree wind, these red flowers
Will drift, love had planted the tree,
Settled him in this famous palace
He'll need a stretch of low land to sleep

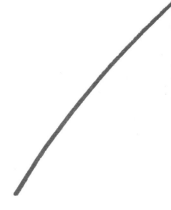

In Love I Have Descended to the Dirt

(1978)

The Girl Named Mungri

With many rocks it has covered the path
The tiny stream that flows past the heart
Across it, houses by a linseed farm
If only you had known the girl named Mungri
You'd like it if you knew how the breeze
Suddenly makes her bunched-up hair fly
Whispering rain, with the flowers dropping
Pollen, the distant mountain-woods of teak
It's not building a home in another's mind
Nor opening the moon's doors and windows
The tiny stream that flows past the heart
Across it, houses by a linseed farm
If only you had known the girl named Mungri

Like a Tiger, the Car

Like a tiger between gardens on both sides
The car bursts the darkness with feral eyes
Burning petrol, racing to the mountains
Speeds and races, stops, winds around the hill
Descends, flaming flowers redden the way
Stomping over them, all those images of grace
The car rages like a tiger through the gardens
Some black men, their drums, the rains, shatter
The night, like rocks, like a meteor shower
Arrogant, angry, unquiet and violent with grief

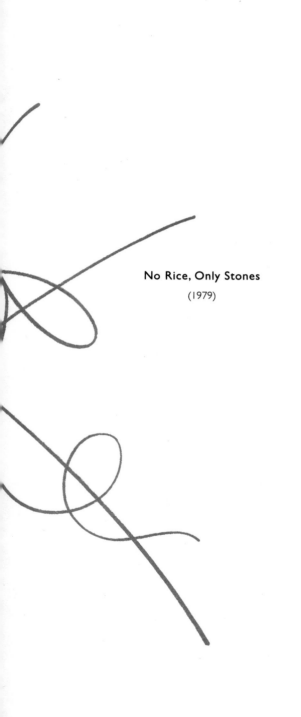

No Rice, Only Stones

(1979)

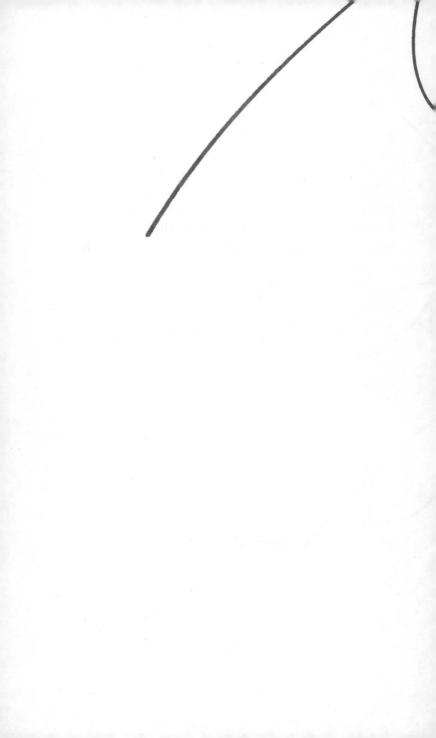

Old New Sorrow

When a man weeps, who's man enough to stop him?
He weeps near the river, he sits by the rock to weep
In the field he weeps alone, his eyes raised to the sky
Who's man enough to stop him? He weeps alone, not with
    others?
When a man weeps, who's man enough to stop him?
Blood bursts from his eyes, blood that sticks
To his glittering clothes, rainwater washes away grime
It cannot coax or coerce the smear of blood to leave
Bloodstains remain on clothes like a retreating
Revolution, how long do clothes take to be torn?

Stay for Some Time

For ten days I've been imprisoned
A false incarceration, Calcutta's streets call,
Trams pass noisily, buses ring as they go past
I see nothing, I hear, I like hearing them

All these Calcutta streets eloquent with garbage
Have boycotted walking, still everyone walks
Only I have no wheels on my feet but chains
I'm like a parrot whose bowl of peas is full
With my beak I peel them, I eat chillies
Guava seeds and kidney beans, I drink water
I depend on these thick shackles on my ankles
It's a happy life. I perch on my rod, singing
To my heart's content, warbling human words
They understand me, and so they tell me, stay
But freedom does not mean wantonness
You are capricious, and so a prisoner
Stay for some time.

Your Ring, Golden Water

(1980)

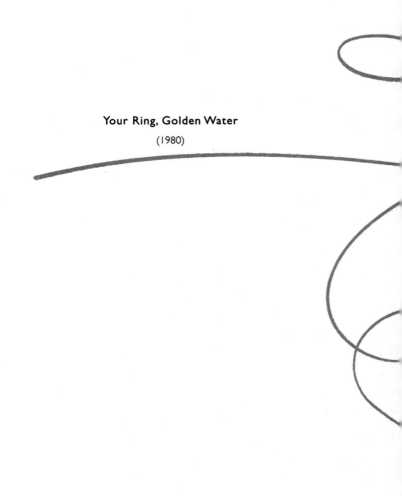

A Blue Nursery Rhyme

Like a blue nursery rhyme the days pass
Just as in the wind, a fragrance soars
So too does some sort of woman's face in my mind
Through open windows, closed doors

Some

Some grass has come away in my fist, some has slipped
Through my fingers, clarifying:
I am not entirely yours

You can do some, and I, some
Some are asexual, some, sexual
You can do some, and I, some
Certainly someone else can do some
Rich man poor man beggar man thief
Someone else can certainly do some of it

Easy

I can just as well let go
This garden, this flower-garden—these pots and pans
I can just as well let go
The main gate, the lotus pond, the broken heart, the house
I can just as well let go
Letting go is very easy, after all
And it's very easy to let them go

• ••

Let Me Look at Them

Uproot the trees, plant them in the garden
All I need is to look at trees
To keep gazing at them
My body craves their green
I desperately need their green to recover

For years I haven't lived in the forest
For years I haven't been to the forest
For years I've been living in the city
The city disease only gulps the green
There's a dearth of green

And so I'm saying, uproot the trees
Plant them in the garden, let me look at them
My eyes desire green
My body desires a green garden
Bring the trees, plant them here

Let me look at them

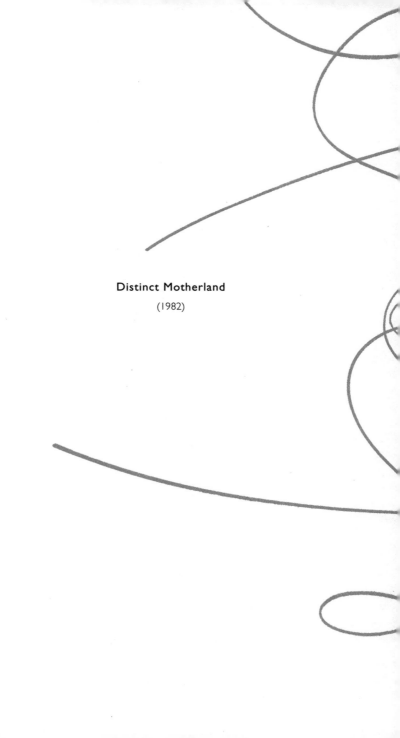

Distinct Motherland

(1982)

To Visit the Forest

There's no fixed day or time to visit the forest
You can go to the jungle whenever you like
Whether to pick leaves or to swing an axe
There's always a generous invitation to the forest
Have you ever walked with the moon in the forest?
Have you seen it sliced by a saw of leaves?
Like a football the moon is poised over the hill
Waiting for the late-night game and the war cries
At these moments you can visit the forest

How Can They?

This time the Gopalpur sea is like a backyard pond
The seashore begins just beneath the veranda
Crabs in a row have created a pattern
Treading on the buttery sand, a sudden flock
Of children towards the water

There's no boat
The catamaran couldn't be launched
Possessed by a demon the waves have thrust it back
On land, where it lies face down, next to it
Sit sunken-cheeked fishermen

Ink from clouds gather in the sky
Dripping on the water, mixing
Liquid rocks crumble in the typhoon
Mad, fierce rain, thunder, froth
The sky mangled by a whip, shattered

For three days now no one has cooked
A meal where the swimming guides live
Unpractised hands held out in the dark lane
They want some money
But they don't talk
How can they?

I Could Go, but Why Should I?

(1982)

I Could Go, but Why Should I?

I think it best to turn around

My hands smeared so black
For so long
Never thought of you, as yours

When I stand by the ravine at night
The moon calls to me, come
When I stand by the Ganga, asleep
The pyre calls to me, come

I could go
I could go either way
But why should I?

I shall kiss my child's face

I'll go
But not just yet
Not alone, unseasonably

A Cat

Very close to pleasure, there's a sick cat
Wrapped in wool and fur, there's a sick cat
It sits close by, this patriotic sick cat
Sits close by to get something, get immortality
Hard to keep when close by, hard to hide in sheets
Hard to hide at home or away, in disease or infatuation
Very close to pleasure, there's a sick cat

Old New Sorrow

I'll ask my old sorrow to visit me today
I sit here, there's some shade, if sorrow sat by my side
I'd like it, I think I'll tell my new sorrow, go away
Wander about in some other garden of happiness
Destroy flowers, set fire to green leaves, ransack the place
After some time, when you're tired, come back
Sit by me.
For now, make room for my old sorrow
It's been in many gardens and homes, slashed and burnt,
And wants to sit by me now. Let it stay a few days.
Let it find peace. Companionship. Come later.
Come afterwards, my new sorrow.

For Just Two Days

It's for just two days that I've left home and come out
I've left home to be on the road for just two days
From the bungalow in the forest you can see down below
A clear current running and the riverbed, a saucer
Both ends have vanished in the hills within the forest
Like a woman's thighs the banks slope down on the plateau
The delicacy of this scene across the valley
Draws me to itself for just two days, not permanently

What's permanent is life at home, within myself, deep within

Say, You Love

I see I'm the only sick person here in this hospital
The rest are all healthy, constantly pacing the corridor
Wandering where they please, pausing at windows, gazing
At birds, having conversations with birds, newspapers
Are not delivered here.
Who gives a damn for the news or the price of cooking oil?
People free of disease here are more valuable than gold
I am sick, and so I am the only one sick of unhappiness
I lie in my bed, I sit when I want, sometimes I stand
In front of the mirror, speak, speak within me,
Whether you be ghost or spirit, speak within me
Speak of love, no matter if it is like a needle
Speak of cruel, negative things, speak within me
Of things like rain, of lightning, of roots
Say, you are well and your illness has left you now
Say, you love and that is why your illness has left you

It's Hard to Walk on the Road

It's hard to walk on the road, I sit on one side
I sit beneath a deep-rooted tree like a dry leaf
Like a leaf I wait, I suffer at the wind's hand
I am afraid because I can fly, I can burn

It's hard to walk on the road, so I sit by the road
I lie like a mound of earth or an ancient rock
Not thoughtless, not for decoration, certainly a rock
Not a useful rock, it's stopped being useful to languish
Not on the road, away from it, by the side of the road
Beneath a deep-rooted tree like a rock

It's hard to walk on the road, so I sit on the roadside

Demolition Is More Valuable than Creation

Who knows how the veranda of cadences will be demolished
The workmen are present, shovel and crowbar are at hand
There's manpower, there are definite orders to demolish
The power to demolish exists, the necessity too

The veranda has found out everyone isn't adept at demolition
Even demolition has its rhythm, its rules and traditions
Crude demolition will make the science of breaking spit on you
And people will say, this is what it's like to destroy
It's ignorance, they say, imbecile, you must learn to demolish
Demolishing beautifully is even more valuable than creating
Now and then.

Cause Me Pain If You Can

Cause me pain if you can, I like to feel pain
Cause me pain, cause me pain—I like to feel pain
Keep the pleasure, live in pleasure, the door's wide open

Under the sky, stupefied by the shimul's passion
Standing on tiptoes at its base I observe the tower
The way a pedestrian pauses beneath a tree

In solitude I gaze at the banner attached to the beautiful

For better or worse the clouds spread across the sky
The wind wraps me in the embrace of its arms
Holds me to its breast, its mouth—'Keep me not in pleasure

Cause me pain if you can, I like to feel pain
Cause me pain, cause me pain—I like to feel pain
I love the thorn of the flower, I love anguish
In blunders, I love sitting on the bank like a rock
So much water in the river, love, gentle blue water
I am afraid.'

Where Does the Sword Belong, Where Have You Put It?

(1983)

Near the Sea

You've crept up to the sea to sit near it like a cat
Hiding your face in your paw so the fish do not suspect
Nor the water, the waves a foam plumage—hide and seek
That is why you're there next to the sea like a cat
Aren't you human? You've spent a long time learning to swim
To swim in the water, swim in the moonlight, in the boat—
You have learnt know to swim but you sit on the seashore
You don't enter the water, I know, the water is deep
Though you sit outside you know the fears lurking within
You've learnt from the shore how the water of the ocean
Drags you in, how hard it drags
Aren't you human? You've spent a long time learning to swim

Even Floods Are Necessary

Sometimes even floods are necessary
Because the soil must also eat at times
The green needs sustenance, silt, evolution
Sometimes even floods are necessary
But not for laments or death, not destruction
Just let the water flood habitations slowly
Let it caress the earth with a layer of silt
Let the water recede from the doorstep
Let it bring and take away rejected food
Let it bring the future, brimming granaries
Sometimes even floods are necessary

Evening in Cox's Bazaar

(1984)

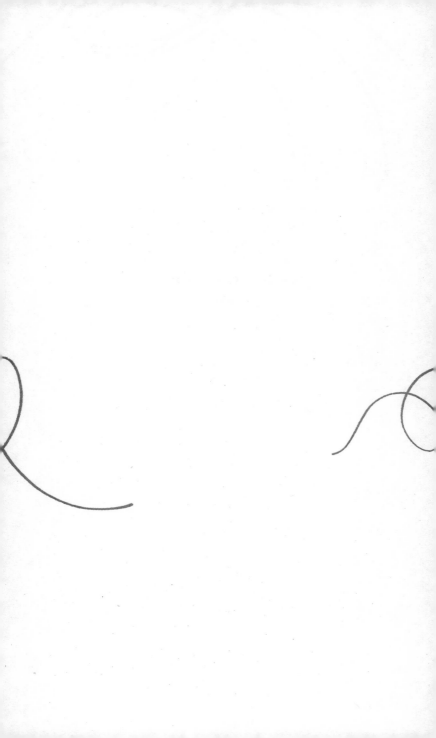

Do Not Come Near Me

My fists are clenched tight, my hand holds poison
Do not come near me, both my hands hold poison
One to give someone and one to take myself
Do not come near me, both my hands hold poison
I am terrifying you I hold poison in my hands

I had a lifespan once, the vulture consumed it
A flower in the roots of my hair, the lice ate it
My palms had lines of the moon, the moonlight
Now, instead, both my hands are full of poison
Do not come near me, both my hands hold poison

Call Them

The wind whirls by the river
Next to the forest
Sweeping up the dust with candour
And dry leaves that have been shed
With all its troops it captures
The forest every day
A bloodless war is waged
On the bank of the river
There are no wails anywhere
Only the ovation of victory
Love and surrender everywhere
Call everyone to the spot

Fire of My Reverence
(1985)

On My Birthday

Some flowers arrived on my birthday
Amid the impossible happiness and laughter and music
A cat climbed up the stairs, counting out
Fifty-two steps of its paws, carefully
A spiral iron staircase, atop the stairs
Unobserved by anyone, atop the black stairs
Only I saw
Its hesitant manner
Its melancholy

Some flowers arrived on my birthday
They've wilted now

Fire of My Reverence

Fire of my reverence
Incinerate me
First, torch the two feet that can no longer move
Then the hands which hold no love or order today
Now icebergs of flowers in the crook of the arms
No more responsibility settling on the shoulders
Burn them in proximity to life
Stop a moment, then destroy
The silent seat of knowledge coloured by truth and lies
Save the pair of eyes
Maybe they still have
Something left to see
When the tears have stopped flowing crush the eyes
Don't burn the garlands and bouquets dishevelled with
    fragrance
A loved touch lives on their bodies
Let them drift on the river freely, wilfully
Fire of my reverence
Incinerate me

To Blossom as Simply as a Flower

To blossom as simply as a flower
Yours was the audacity to bloom
Yours was the glory to bloom
You've been gone somewhere for a while
My loudest calls do not bring you out
I have scoured your neighbourhood
You've been gone somewhere for a while
I will see you blossoming again
See you blooming like a flower again
You've been gone somewhere for a while

In the Evening

In the evening the river song seems slower
After a long time
The sandbank rises messily
Sand
Blue ink from the forest
Has flown into the river
In the evening
The river song seems slower
The river was there in the afternoon, morning too
There was a swift current
Now beneath the blanket of the fog-smeared evening
Slowness comes
The unearthly boat drifts
Who are those who walk on the dam
Of the moon?
They are guarding the boat

Prison

The forest of fawns feels like a prison
The forest of fawns like a harsh prison
For leaves have fallen in winter
Threaded with tender green leaves
Even today the forest isn't filled with trees
The forest of fawns feels like a prison
The forest of fawns like a harsh prison

The Bridge

An island's surfaced in the river
A bridge stands in the middle
Just one bank? Stay on both
The island is mysterious now
You have so much time
Stay
In the river an island's surfaced
A bridge stands in the middle

Ajitesh

Your face made me think it was raining somewhere
Beneath your ascetic brow your eyes were like pools
The palm-leaf hut by the lake built with much effort
The luxuriant yet delicate tower of the tree
You had nothing to do with this fragile existence

With a voice of thunder you turned towards the clouds
You must accept this invitation to our drought!
You held life in your arms with such love
Some rocks, some hardness, cracked from its ache
You threatened, we will farm this fissured stone,
Clumps of love flowers will bloom, I want leaves too,
You said the garden would have mountains of overwhelmed
    green

We learnt from you how to love in a different way, by ourselves
Only you knew how to contain the turbulent winds within
    your arms
We would be afraid, you could realize the impossible with ease
Whenever I close my eyes today I see you do not fit that bed
With a meaningful smile you made death tie the knot with life

So effortlessly
Was it necessary?
Was this ceremony needed? Was the understated melodrama
    required?

The sharp wonder of a comet left us suddenly in this manner
You were as transparently beautiful as the deepening night
I never cared for your stories of living in happiness
You vaulted over the barbed wire, inevitably, to win a life of war
Even mauled and lacerated you were as derisive as a lion
I curse the life-giving air that has left your body hollow today

Calcutta, at Dawn

Like a tram at dawn, love is cranked up
In people's minds and bodies. Winter has shifted
Unloading bales of grain at the warehouse in the south.
The truck races away to the north, laden with
Sorrowful hay. Ceaselessly.

A slow light blossoms like flowers
In a pot, in the veranda.
Even smeared with Calcutta's calumny, they bloom
They bloom and they die, at this moment, hundreds of children
Nothing is beautiful any more when we remember this
A bitter Calcutta is no longer alluring at dawn
After a wakeful night, on slow footsteps,
People return home. Some
Leave home to go out.

The boy leads the old man by the hand to look for peanuts
Sifting through the aged leaves the old man finds a few
His childhood wriggles within him like a jumpy fish
The sun awakes, the sun rises

Calcutta changes its clothes in every home to go to work

Like Support, Love

Like support, love stood at the door
—You said you were well, is this
What you meant by well
Cries of shame split two countries apart
—To east and to west
—You said you were well, is this what you meant by well
From useless acts useful acts are born
Ghosts and spirits are born, heaven and hell
From useless acts useful acts are born

Here's the Figure in Stone

(1987)

The Boy Wraps Sleeping Arms

The boy wraps sleeping arms round his cruel father
Who's always travelling to cities, forests, remote lands
Constantly rushing from one place to another
I'll be back soon, he says, and goes away abruptly

The child won't go along, his arms have grasped the man
It's even possible the father will ignore these bonds
And leave at the dead of night, forsaking everything
Memories will be left, the warmth of a memorable bed
Why does he do this? His son does not understand
What mad attraction, what company takes him away?
What disease is this that no medicine can cure?
The boy wraps sleeping arms round his cruel father

For Biren-da

I had wanted a single drop
Of light just like you
So that if possible I could
Shine in it again
But you did not stay
Today in the room within
All the light that I need
Is in your heart alone

Wake Me Up

(1989)

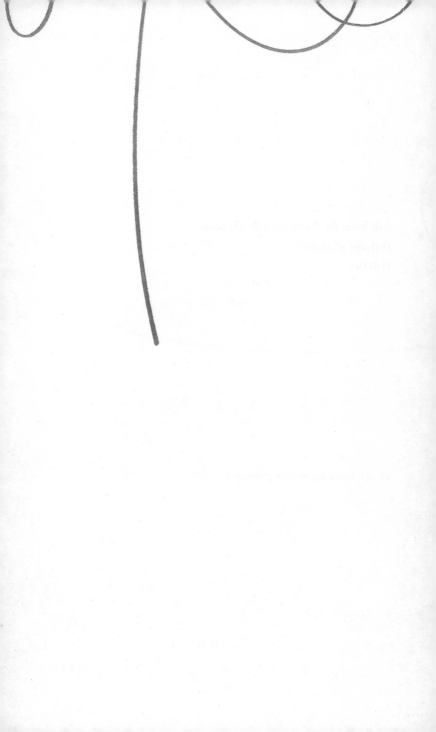

It Will End, This Is How It Ends

I lit it a long time ago
Now it really will go out
Ash from the flames will fly far away
Perhaps all desire
Will die
This is how it ends
The wood rots, decay sets in
So this is how it ends
Sometimes the days will pass
Dragging our feet, bodies
No matter how
One day they
Will burn down
Is there anything left to say?
To the man it's all lies
To the man it's nothing but lies

Then Let It Be

His face is smudged by a touch of soot.

The black smoke rising through the chimney
From the burning wick has turned to soot
And smeared itself with care on his face

There is no water anywhere now
Only tears, and then, just a drop
Can it be used to wipe the soot away?
There isn't much time to spare

Then let it be, let the soot remain
Let it drip from the face on the heart

Draws a Picture, Rips It Up

(1991)

The Plant Speaks

I enter the plant to sit inside
Every morning and evening
I water every plant, the flower gives
Plants in return
This exchange goes on, unspoken
In gentle love
A love plants and humans understand
And no one else
I enter the plant to sit inside
Every morning and evening
Not all of them are plants
Weeds grow too
They have to be uprooted with a hoe
Plants live happily
To live happily plants point them out
Casually
Uprooting weeds saddens me
Even they have flowers
Maybe not the lineage that the sunflower
Possesses
But still they have settled in our garden
Out of love
Giving flowers of many hues and forms without

Needing water
They have to be uprooted for the plants
To live happily
I enter the plant to sit inside, the plant
Speaks to me

I Lie by the Lidder

Pahalgam Valley, I am stretched out by the Lidder
The river bubbles, sometimes a hailstorm breaks
Like snow the hailstones drop on the grass
A white and silent layer of ice, tinged with green
Here the winter chill grows like a wild hill
The valley is covered by golf courses, temples, mosques
Pahalgam Valley, I am stretched out by the Lidder
The river bubbles, sometimes a hailstorm breaks

Countless dreams pass by during my repose
None of them painful, all serene, luxurious
Camp-beds, meat curries, a fountain of Scotch
The window shows youngsters fishing for trout
I wonder how to match this scene with what's back home
I'll try camping out all night in my yard

Safdar Hashmi

For bringing the language of your heart to your lips
They murdered you
India wants much more blood
India will fill its rivers and lakes
With the blood of plain speakers like you
This India will fertilize trees with it
Hashmi Hashmi
We will not give our lives as easily
No matter how much India wants it

Some Ties Remain

(1996)

Elegy

(In memory of Samaresh Basu)

We met on the appointed day of pain
Yet what a smile was waiting to greet me
A regal smile was waiting to greet me
Describable on the appointed day of pain
How do I describe it, you sat there
Isolated, impassive—the doors and walls
Parted, let them recede—the wind first
Nobody intimate nearby, you sat there
Beneath a sky full of shade you sat there

I heard that waves rose in the sea then
A meagre lifespan, how long could you live
Under its careless control, and so you died
It was you the magic of twilight chose to touch
The young devotee's face was turned today
Into Ramkinkar's, where passion was all

Come Back Malobika

Malobika, go no more over there
Talk no more to that young man
What do you say to him?—With him!
Malobika! Do you know if salt lines the grass?
I sit before a forest of deodars
Come back Malobika, how delicious this is, life is
Come back Malobika, go no more with that young man
In Santiniketan I have seen the palash bloom
Come back Malobika
I will adorn you with those palash blooms
I will adorn you with vermilion dust
I will adorn you with my love
Come back Malobika
Go no more with the young man
Here clouds and castle resonate wondrously
Come back Malobika, make a wish, come back at once

Kinship

In the garden petunias have bloomed
Rows of jasmines and geraniums
The lilies have blossomed beautifully
And clusters of white hibiscus
I sit among them in the evening
With them too, a kinship grows
I know their joys, none of their sorrows
With them only a kinship grows

It Won't Be Long

There's a fire in the eastern sky
It must be put out
It has to be put out somehow
Else danger looms over men women children
The tree will die if the axe hits the roots
Human beings are not weeds
The victory of the human heart
Will be in jeopardy

Animals will not recognize humans as human
Danger is imminent, unless
You can do something at once
You have to do whatever you can at once
It's already too late
The wind is rising
It won't be long before the fire spreads to the edges

Dot Dot Dash Dash

(1996)

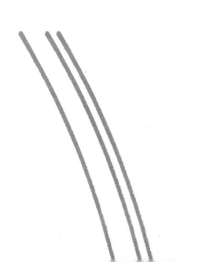

Just Me

I had meant to race along
Like a river
I had meant to be as still
As a tree

But suddenly the bird called out
A solitary bird like me
So, to let you know, I freed my arm
And ran away to you

Before I came I set on fire
All those rocks, the enormous rock, and all the way
To the door

The Dinosaur's Fossil

To view the dinosaur's fossil, the geologist
Goes to Hyderabad, at the Nizam's museum
The dinosaur's body lies in fragments
Fossilized doubts have been excavated

The powerful dinosaur must continue to suffer
Even after death, life won't let him die
A specialist who can put the bones together
Is on his way to the city of Hyderabad

Uncollected Poems

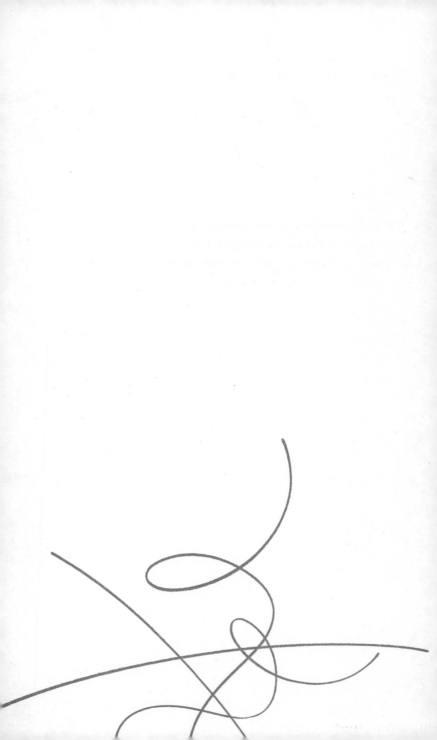

Like a Necklace around a Mountain

Fiery beautiful like a necklace on the mountain
I can see it from my forest bungalow
It is the end of winter now, spring is beginning
All the branches are covered with leaves
Their clenched hands fill with tender green
Dry leaves burn beneath, leaves fly,
Some of them, the stream flows below in vain
In vain the stream flows far below
It cannot put out the fiery beautiful necklace
The mountain wears it round its neck instead

In My Head I Have Gone Far Away

In my head I have gone far away—to return, I'll have to
    be reborn
And walk as soon as I am born
If I keep walking
I might reach where I had started
There's not just one road, after all
Still, all of them are tied to the same beginning and end
To the two sides of the river
People living on one side, nobody on the other
On both sides there are banks, crossing, journeys, warp
    and weft
It takes two lives
In my head it takes two lives

The Desert

The woman had seemed a bit like a load-bearing camel
Yet the afternoon would say, to young men,
She was the best choice in the easy, dwindling light
Perhaps all this is in close proximity to untruth
Else it is lying far away, subservient to truth

Am I not a young man, ancestor? Experience has made
Ancestors of us. A bit like camels, the women will leave
One desert for another. We are delighted when
The current of peace next door trembles,
Foolish desert travellers, who will say they aren't blind?

Death Will Come Later

Death will come later. Death will not come today, this very night.
After a very long time I am in proximity with death
I have lived a long time, may I live longer still
Death will come later.
Living unashamedly for some time is possible, isn't it?
Such shame in dying, even if the man lived to a hundred
The man doesn't know how shameful it is to keep living

I Need

Let there be a faint breeze, so I can bare my body
Let there be a little rain, so I can hold out my hand
Come forward one step at a time
That's all I need to leave home and step on the road

These are things I need to do now

Let there be a little money, so I can climb on it
Let there be a little pleasure, so I can flow on it
The way people climb mountains or go down to the river
Now I want possession of all of these

That's all I need to leave home and step on the road
These are things I need to do now

The Cat

The cat came into the garden
Nosed about inside broken eggshells
Tasted bricks, tasted leaves
The cat came into the garden
Came in suddenly

Got no water, nothing to slaughter
Could not find a pretext
To die
Cooking some stale dirt rice
And doing its hair in a bun
It fell at the strike of a paw

The cat went out of the garden
Went out suddenly

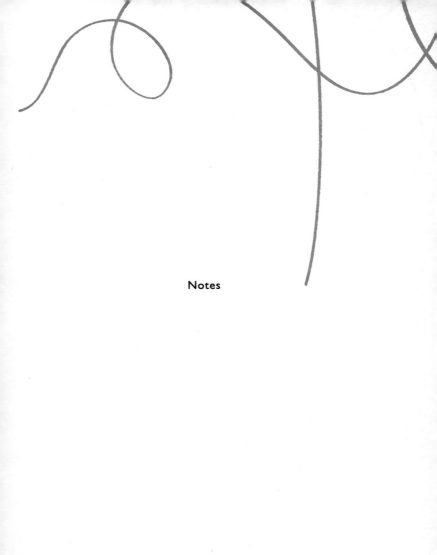

Notes

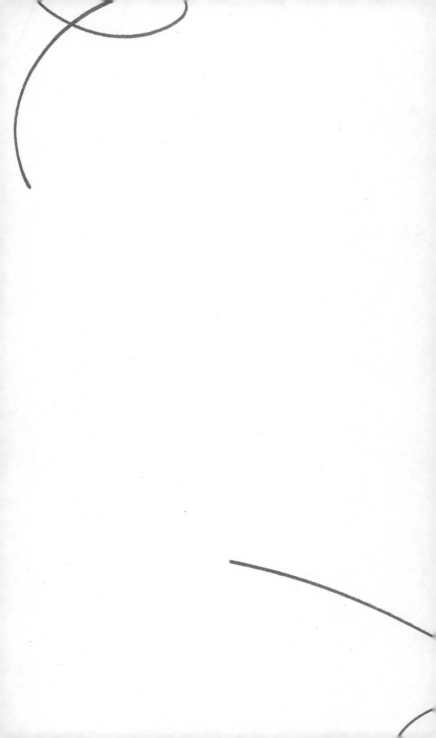

Page 9

sal forest: Sal, or *Shorea robusta*, is a species of tree native to the Indian subcontinent. Generally the predominant tree in forests in which it grows, sal is especially common in the drier parts of Assam, Jharkhand, Odisha and West Bengal.

Page 27

Palm Avenue: A street in the South Calcutta neighbourhood of Ballygunge. At the time the poem was written, this was considered a wealthy locality and it often features in 1960–70s left-leaning literature and cinema as a symbol of urban bourgeois society.

Calcutta Maidan: A large park in the heart of Calcutta, the Maidan (literally, 'open field') encompasses numerous playgrounds, including the famous cricket venue Eden Gardens, several football stadia and the Calcutta Race Course as well as iconic colonial-era buildings such as the Victoria Memorial, the Governor's House and the National Library. A centre of leisure and entertainment for the city, it is often called 'the breathing lungs of Calcutta'.

ration card: A card given to Indian citizens to bring them under the national food-security scheme called the Public Distribution System. Started soon after country's Independence in 1947, the scheme's objective is to reach heavily subsidized essential food and non-food items to India's poor.

A ration card, hence, has often been used as a symbol of the lower socioeconomic class in urban India.

'*Sri*': Often transliterated as *shree* or *shri*, this term is used in the Indian subcontinent as a polite form of address equivalent to the English 'Mister'.

Page 31

Kumortuli: The traditional potter's quarter in North Calcutta where clay idols are manufactured by hand for numerous Hindu religious occasions, especially the annual Durga puja festival in autumn. The clay idols of gods and goddesses are decorated with elaborate, glittery, flamboyant costumes to which the poet refers.

Page 37

Platero: The name of a little donkey, the main character of *Platero y yo* (Platero and I, 1914), one of most popular works of the Nobel Prize–winning Spanish writer Juan Ramón Jiménez (1881–1958). For more, see pp. *xviii–xix* of the introduction to this volume.

Page 40

Moheen's horses: A reference to Jibanananda Das' poem 'Ghora' (Horse/s) from the volume *Shaat-ti Tara-r Timir* (The Darkness of Seven Stars, 1948) in which the second line reads: 'Moheen's horses graze on the horizon of autumnal moonlight'. 'Moheen-er Ghoraguli' (Moheen's Horses) was also the name of a popular alternative Bengali rock band of the 1970s; the name was inspired by the same line in Das' poem. For more on Das, see note 6 on p. *xix*.

Shaheed Minar: An iconic Calcutta structure, the 48-mtere tall
Shaheed Minar (Martyr's Tower) was constructed in 1828
in the memory of Sir David Ochterlony, a commander of
the British East India Company. In 1969, the Indian
government rededicated it to all martyrs of the Indian
Independence Movement. The area around the Shaheed
Minar has been the venue of numerous significant politi-
cal meetings and demonstrations.

Ritwik: The poem is dedicated to Ritwik Ghatak (1925–76), a
Bengali filmmaker and scriptwriter best known for his
meticulous yet dramatic depiction of social reality in films
such as *Ajantrik* (The Un-mechanical, 1955), *Meghe Dhaka
Tara* (The Cloud-Capped Star, 1960), *Komal Gandhar* (E-
flat, 1961) and *Jukti Takko aar Goppo* (Reason, Debate and
Stories, 1974). A radical leftist, Ghatak was fearlessly and
decidedly political in his work, and greatly respected by
the left-leaning intelligentsia of the time. Marked by an
obsessive preoccupation with the 1947 Partition of India,
Ghatak's cinema is highly regarded for its powerful repre-
sentations of the trauma of this event.

Mikir Hills: A group of hills to the south of the Kaziranga
National Park in North-East India, well known for its pop-
ulations of one-horned rhinoceroses and elephants.

Page 136

Gopalpur: A former commercial port, Gopalpur is a popular
beach town and tourist destination in eastern Indian state
of Odisha.

Page 146

shimul: A common Asian cotton-producing tree, the shimul, or
Bombax ceiba, is famous for its brilliant red flowers that
bloom in spring.

Page 151

Cox's Bazar: A city and fishing port in southern Bangladesh,
Cox's Bazar is the country's most popular tourist destina-
tion, known for its unbroken 120-kilometre-long sandy
beach, the longest in the world.

Page 163

Ajitesh: Dedicated to Ajitesh Bandyopadhyay (1933–83), a
renowned actor, playwright, director and leftist political
activist, who, along with Shambhu Mitra and Utpal Dutt,
is considered one of the doyens of post-Independence-era
Bengali theatre. Revered for his thunderous voice and
powerful performances on stage and screen, his early
death at the age of 50 shocked the Bengali cultural world.

Page 170

Biren-da: Most probably a reference to poet and leftist political
activist Birendra (or, in short, Biren) Chattopadhyay
(1920–85), *da* being the common Bengali term of endear-
ment for an elder brother. With a palpably acute political
consciousness and a strong sense of social responsibility,

his poetry explores, in starkly beautiful verse, the everyday struggles of the common man. His volumes of poetry include *Visa Office-r Shamne* (In Front of the Visa Office, 1967), *Vietnam: Bharatbarsha* (Vietnam: India, 1969) and *Amar Jajner Ghora* (The Sacrificial Horse, 1985).

Page 179

Pahalgam Valley . . . the Lidder: A popular tourist destination in the North Indian state of Jammu and Kashmir, at the height of more than 2,000 metres, Pahalgam Valley nestles the beautiful River Lidder, which is a tributary of the River Jhelum further south.

Page 180

Safdar Hashmi: A communist playwright and director, Safdar Hashmi (1954–89) was best known across India for his political street theatre. On 2 January 1989, while performing his street play *Halla Bol* (Raise Your Voice!) in Jhandapur in the North Indian state of Uttar Pradesh, Hashmi was murdered by members of the ruling Indian National Congress party.

Page 183

Samaresh Basu: A major writer of Bengali fiction and children's literature, Basu (1924–88) is considered the most representative storyteller of Bengal's suburban life, as distinct from other well-known authors who depicted rural society or the urban middle class. His notable novels include *Bibar* (Hole, 1965) and *Prajapati* (Butterfly, 1967), both of which were temporarily banned on charges of obscenity, as well as the award-winning *Shambo* (1980).

Ramkinkar: A reference to Ramkinkar Baij (1906–80), Bengali sculptor and painter, and one of the leading figures of modernism in Indian art. Samaresh Basu's last and unfinished work, titled *Dekhi Nai Phire* (I Haven't Looked Back), is a meticulously researched study of Baij's life and work. It was serialized in the Bengali *Desh* magazine in 1987–88, accompanied by extensive illustrations by another major contemporary artist Bikash Bhattacharya.

Page 184

palash: A species of deciduous tree, *Butea monosperma*, native to South and South-East Asia. Known as 'the flame of the forest' for its large and brilliant red-orange flowers, palash is widely referenced in Bengali literature, especially by Rabindranath Tagore, as a symbol of springtime and vivacity.

Page 190

Goes to Hyderabad, at the Nizam's museum: The Nizam was the monarch of the prosperous Hyderabad State in South India from 1724 till 1948, when the Indian Army deposed him and annexed his kingdom to the newly independent Union of Indian. The Nizam Museum is located in the Purani Haveli (Old Palace), the sovereign's erstwhile residence in the city of Hyderabad, Telengana, and houses souvenirs, mementos and miscellaneous belongings of the last Nizam, Osman Ali Khan (1886–1967), who, at the time of his deposition, was one of the wealthiest men in the world.